LET ME SEE YOUR BODY TALK!

The Handbook for Sales Professionals

J. Merelle Rodrigo

June-

Continued Success

This book is dedicated to Paul Garramone
who taught me so much of what I know
about listening and speaking.

Acknowledgements

There is an old saying that goes, "Show me who your friends are and I will tell you who you are." This saying very much applies to me. I have been blessed with the love and encouragement of my family, in particular, my mother, Merle Rodrigo and my husband, Jack Garramone. My dear son, Gregory, who brings me so much joy, has always been my motivator.

This book would not have been possible were it not for the very talented presenters who gave me the gift of their time, experience and interest. In particular, I would like to thank Bob Astley, Barry Triller, Bob Barr, Dwight Powell, John Lanni and Patricia King. My time with you gave me insight into your personal characters and the reasons behind your success.

To my photographer, Susan Mitchell, thank you for capturing the impact body language makes. You had the added challenge of making a silk purse from a sow's ear. Well done.

To Irene Gesza, my proofreader, who respected the integrity of my work and taught me to take greater care in its ultimate expression.

To all of you who have lent your support, I thank you from the very bottom of my heart.

Contents

Introduction

My brother–in–law, Paul Garramone, was deaf. He couldn't hear and he couldn't speak. Yet he taught me more about listening, speaking and reading the non–verbal communication of those around me than any of my professors. He taught me the difference between the active art of listening and the passive act of hearing. Paul, although he never heard me, always listened to me.

I have written this book as a handbook for people in sales. I very deliberately called it a handbook because that is where I suggest you keep it — close at hand. Don't read it only once and put it on the shelf of your office or your home library. It won't be an effective tool if it stays on your library shelf — long forgotten.

Take this handbook with you on your sales calls. Read it in your car between appointments. Read it at lunch. Discuss it with your colleagues. Work with it every day. Keep it in your computer bag or with your paperwork. Keep it where you can see it. Read it and refer to it daily.

This is a handbook for Sales Professionals. The examples and references throughout the book are customized to assist Sales Professionals. This said, however, let me explain that successful Sales Professionals have learned the art of Persuasion. To persuade others to act, and act *now*, is something that all human beings, everywhere, do every day of our lives. We are all in sales to one extent or another.

Whether you are counselling a married couple or recommending a course of treatment, you are *selling* your ideas, thoughts, concepts and expectations for behaviour every day. I worked as a Probation Officer for six years. I got some of my best sales training by helping those clients adopt a pro–social lifestyle. I was *selling* the non–criminal way of life and many of the people to whom I was selling *didn't want to buy.*

Persuading others to adopt your point of view, to accept what you are saying is the challenge of Professionals in all walks of life. In order to be most effective, in order to have the highest impact, in order to enjoy the greatest success, the key is to improve not just *what you say* but *how you say it.*

Body language, in all its complexities, is the key to mastering the art of Persuasion. Learning to speak with your body ensures that people not only hear what you are saying but listen to what you say.

Learn to use your body to project a more professional image, to speak with more confidence and authority, to influence others. Your sales will soar, your confidence will overflow, and you will be amazed at what you are truly capable of achieving.

CHAPTER 1:

The Hidden Messages in Body Language

It was a Saturday morning in March of this year when I tasted bitter humiliation and felt the heat of shame stain my face with tears. I had just left the Honda Dealership in my city and I was upset. I felt outraged and humiliated.

Earlier that morning, my husband and I decided that we would look at purchasing another vehicle as the lease was close to expiring on his current car, and he wished to change the make and model of his car to a Honda Pilot. We drove over to the Honda dealership and while he made a quick trip to the bathroom (bladder control becomes a problem after 50!) I walked around the showroom.

And then I saw it! I saw the car of my dreams, the car that took my breath away. Everything about it — the shape, the colour, the model, the make — made my heart sing. It was an S–2000 and it was absolutely beautiful. I walked around it, maybe six or seven times. It was a low–slung, two–seater convertible polished to perfection and I can tell you that *my* body language was screaming, "*I am interested in this vehicle! I love this vehicle!*"

This was a vehicle which cost nearly $50,000. The commission on this sale, with all the trimmings would have made many a salesperson's mouth water, or so you would think. The dealership was not busy. I was one of six or seven customers on the showroom floor. *Not one salesperson in the dealership made eye contact with me. Not one salesperson made the effort to say "Hello" or that they would be "Right with me." No one smiled. No one read* ***my*** *body language.* I looked at that car for well over five minutes and my husband joined me and admired the car as well. Anybody reading our body language would have seen the excitement and passion and energy that emanated from our joint enthusiasm over this vehicle.

No one approached us. We stood there for close to ten minutes together and not one Sales Professional or Honda employee so much as welcomed us or made any move towards us. Now, just in case you are wondering, I did have a shower that morning! Both my husband and I were clean and appropriately dressed for a Saturday morning. We weren't attired in business suits, but we were casually and neatly dressed. Not that it would have mattered, because no one even made eye contact with us. My efforts at attracting a salesperson to us were unsuccessful. Not one of them came towards us. We left.

As I sat in our car at the Honda parking lot, humiliated and embarrassed, Jack said, "We both work too hard for our money to spend it in there." He was right. And I learned what was to be a very valuable and important lesson. It is the lesson that inspired me to write this book.

Body language is **the most important ingredient** in communication. For Sales Professionals, body language is the heart and soul of communication and success. Whether you are selling life insurance or lingerie, cosmetics or computers, clothing or cars, health care supplements or health insurance, children's toys or kitchen accessories, mastering your own body language and learning to read the body language of those around you will increase your closing ratio.

Why?

Communication is based on two parts: *verbal* and *non–verbal.* When companies hire and train Sales Professionals, they focus mainly on the verbal component of communication. Countless hours are spent indoctrinating newly hired salespeople on, you guessed it, product. Hour after hour, the features, benefits and integral components of product are drilled into heads of Sales Professionals until they can re–iterate with amazing accuracy all the details of how the product functions and benefits the prospective purchaser. And although knowing your product is an extremely important function of sales, an even *more* important and less utilized component is *knowing how to most effectively communicate with your customer.*

Non–verbal communication is the key to unlocking the gaps in communication created by words and helps to break through the resistance people have to "being sold." People don't like to "be sold." How would you feel if someone said to you, "I can sell you this car in less than ten minutes?" Chances are, you wouldn't like it. We have an unconscious aversion to being sold and, as a result, Sales Professionals have to overcome the resistance many buyers have to being sold anything. Do people need and benefit from life insurance? Yes, but do they like having it sold to them? No, definitely not. As a result, focusing on product and "what to say to the customer" is a flawed strategy unless it is combined with the all–important use of body language.

IMPORTANCE OF BODY LANGUAGE

There are things your body can say that your mouth would *never* say. For example, how would it sound if you told your client that you were compassionate, intelligent, well–read, articulate, have high attraction power and were interested in them as well as interested in how best your product would suit them?

Here is a lesson I learned from my grandmother as a little girl.

Whenever I would talk too much about myself, especially if I boasted of my accomplishments or some little thing that I had done, she would say that I sounded like "a monkey praising its own tail." And this is the mistake that many salespeople make. Many salespeople work off the mistaken premise that *selling is telling.*

Rule #1:

Selling isn't telling.

Selling has less to do with speaking and more to do with body language: how you sit; where you sit; your eye contact; your tone; the loudness of your voice; pauses, silences, hesitations, rate of speech; inflections of voice; your facial expressions; your posture; your gestures; your use of physical distance. These non–verbal modes of communicating say far more than words could ever tell.

The purpose of this book is to improve your non–verbal communication, whether you are speaking to one person or one thousand people. It is my intention to help you get comfortable with using your body consciously when you speak because your body talks to people as loudly as your words.

Body language is used by public speakers to hold people's attention, to captivate people, to mesmerize people. Professional speakers are mainly in the business of selling. What are we selling? *Hot air.* If you think your product is hard to move, imagine how hard it is to sell hot air! Time and time again, I have watched how simple gestures, silences and inflections in tone have brought people to tears, or brought people to their feet (even better) clapping and laughing.

Your body is the most powerful tool in your sales kit — much more powerful than a brochure, than your laptop, much more powerful than all the sales illustrations that you printed off before leaving your office. Your body is the key to unlocking the resistance that your clients routinely use to avoid being sold. What you do to master your body and understand the power behind your movements will rocket you to greater success than you would ever have believed possible.

I am stunned, amazed, disappointed and often angered by the sheer number of incompetent, ineffective and poorly trained salespeople. My experience at Honda was but one of many instances of poor service.

It is clear to me that sales training should include a sector on improving the body language of Sales Professionals as well as reading the body language of their customers. This type of training must be practiced *regularly* because adults learn by doing. It is not enough for you to just read this book. Practicing the skills that are taught in this book is just as important as reading them.

At the end of each chapter, I have included behaviour modification exercises. The purpose of these practical exercises is to enhance and improve your skill level.

ROLES AND UNIFORMS

We lead such busy lives these days. We are parents, children to aging parents, spouses, employers, employees, volunteers, athletes, and sports enthusiasts. The uniform we wear for each of these roles is different, based on the expected set of behaviours for that role.

What is the uniform you wear in your role as a Sales Professional? What should you wear? What shouldn't you wear? How can you best project your efficiency, your professionalism and your personal integrity by the clothes you wear?

Everyone who occupies a role in our society has a uniform. Police Officers, Surgeons, Nurses, Judges, Chief Executive Officers and Firefighters all have a uniform. That uniform serves two purposes:

1. Members of the public can identify them immediately and interact with them accordingly.

2. They behave in a manner that reflects the uniform.

Sales Professionals also have uniforms. These uniforms reflect their level of commitment to their role. The more time and effort they take with their overall appearance, the greater the impact they will have on their customers. Understanding the impact your appearance has on your customers is key.

Uniforms are powerful. Not only do they affect the public, they *influence the wearer.* Your behaviour when you are wearing a well–pressed suit is different than when you are wearing your pyjamas. Dressing the role influences acting the role.

CHAPTER 1
BEHAVIOUR MODIFICATION EXERCISES

1. Learn to watch and interpret the body language of others at all times. Go to a clothing retailer that you have never been to before. Within 30 seconds, spot who the manager is and which salesperson is the top salesperson on the floor. Ask and check your answers.
2. Pretend to lose your voice. Go to a restaurant and order lunch *without saying a word.* Use body language, exclusively, to order lunch. Learn how to *exaggerate to communicate.* What you will learn from this exercise is how much you already know about body language. This also teaches you the level of body language you should use when speaking in public.
3. Use body language to get a loved one to give you a hug without verbally asking. Chances are, you used proxemics and kinesics, words which may be meaningless now, but will be examined in depth in later chapters.
4. Tell a joke or anecdote. At the punch line, throw your head back and laugh. Notice the impact that your laughter has on the laughter of your audience. Laughter is infectious.
5. When you are stopped at a red light in traffic, get the person in the car next to you to smile.
6. Watch an unfamiliar movie with the sound completely muted. Can you guess at the story line? Who is the protagonist (the good guy), and who is the antagonist (the bad guy)? Watch the movie again, this time with the sound. Were you right?

CHAPTER 2:

Clothes and Colour Language — The Sale Before the Sale

"Every time I interact with someone,
I am telling them something about who I am."
— Anonymous

We have all heard the term "dress for success" and yet I have seen many a Sales Professional dress for a sale as though they were playing a round of golf or dancing at a night club as opposed to selling their product. The way you dress has an enormous impact on your mood, your self-confidence, they way you project yourself, your authority and the power and energy that emanates from you. Your body is a very powerful tool, and the better it is dressed, the more powerful a tool it is.

The second most important rule in sales is:

Rule #2:
Salespeople don't have dress-down days or business casual days.

The way you look impacts the way you project confidence, authority and success. It is very challenging and difficult to look competent and successful in creased and wrinkled pants that have coffee stains down the front of them and a t–shirt that doesn't look like it has ever been introduced to an iron.

During the summer months, many companies introduce a Business Casual policy, and many times, this policy is abused by the employees. Business Casual does not mean "hootchie tops." For those of you who don't know what a "hootchie top" is, it is a tight–fitting top which molds to the curves of a woman's body and often stops just before her navel, such that her midriff is plainly visible, as is the piercing in her navel and the tattoo on the small of her back. A fashion statement, unquestionably, but not at all what a Sales Professional should wear to the office or to a client interview.

In this section, I will outline some of the dos and don'ts of business dress for Sales Professionals, with the information divided into separate catagories for men and women.

BUSINESS DRESS FOR MEN

1. **Always wear a blazer, preferably dark blue or black.** Many Sales Professionals spend untold hours in their vehicles driving from one sales call to another. A dark blue or black blazer does not show the wrinkles across the back of the blazer caused by long hours in the car. Still, remove the blazer before you sit down in your car, hang it in the back with a special blazer hanger, and wear it only once you get to your destination. Remove it again, just before you get into the car, and re–hang it. Get into the habit of doing this and your blazer will always be wrinkle–free and crease–free when you wear it to a sales call. Not only that, but you will extend the life of your blazer.
2. **Do not remove your blazer once you reach your destination, no matter how warm you are.** A blazer, especially a dark coloured one, connotes authority. You should wear a blazer, especially if your client is wearing one, and keep it on even if your client removes his or her blazer. In fact, if the client is meet-

ing you at your office, keep your blazer on and encourage your client to take his blazer off. This immediately puts the salesperson in a position of confidence and authority, but the client would be hard–pressed to explain why. A blazer is not only elegant in appearance, it is a high–authority garment.

3. **Do not wear cream–coloured pants on the day you have a lot of sales calls.** As I mentioned earlier, many Sales Professionals drive from one sales call to another. In preparation for their long hours in the car, they arm themselves with a good cup of coffee and some good music. Sometimes, they drink their coffee and eat a toasted bagel, laden with cream cheese or soaked in butter. Sadly there is a law of physics that clearly states that when you are wearing light–coloured pants, your coffee will spill down your pants, and the butter from your bagel will drip onto your shirt. Wearing a stained outfit does impair your body language because you are consciously aware of the stains and take pains to hide it, thus detracting from the power and energy that should be emanating from your body.
4. **Golf shirts are for golf courses.** What you wear impacts the way you feel about yourself. We all wear different hats on any given day. We are fathers, sons, husbands, athletes, employees and employers. And what we wear impacts the way we behave. Think back to how differently you felt when you wore a well–cut dark suit as opposed to wearing track pants and a sweatshirt. The clothes you wear have a direct effect on how well you project yourself and the confidence that radiates from you. I interviewed Barry Triller, an Executive Vice–President at Sun Life Financial, and he recalled an incident when he and his team were negotiating the purchase of the Canadian business operations of another major insurer. One Saturday morning, after a particularly stressful week, the respective negotiators met for another long session. While the other negotiators came dressed infor-

mally, in jeans and casual shirts, Barry had all the members of his team dress in sharp, dark suits. That morning, he handed each member a new tie that he had purchased just for the occasion. Barry's team was dressed in well–pressed, dark suits, crisp shirts and brand new ties, while the other team wore jeans and casual shirts. Needless to say, Barry's team won the negotiations. The key here is they *made the sale before the sale.* Their collective attire shook the confidence of the other negotiators. Barry's group had won even before they started the negotiations. Wearing a golf shirt and golf pants to work sends conflicting messages to your brain. Dressing casually has you behaving casually. Selling is always a game of negotiating. Dressing in a business–like fashion when you are in front of clients enhances your negotiating power. People have asked me whether dressing down is okay on days when they're making phone calls and doing administration work. My answer is always, **NO!** The success of your telephone calls, especially if you are calling clients, is enhanced by your business appearance. Your tone of voice and the confidence with which you speak is also enhanced by your appearance. You will not spend countless hours by the water cooler chatting about yesterday's game. You will be more efficient, organized, and productive on the days that you "dress for success" as opposed to "dress down."

5. **Keep jewellery to a minimum.** If you own a great number of rings, ensure that you only wear one of them when you are dressing for business. Preferably, wear a thin gold band on the ring finger of your left hand. Keep the other rings, particularly the ones that have diamonds or other jewels on them, at home. Your clients should not be distracted from what you are saying by your rings twinkling in the light. Neither should clients be thinking, "Does he get paid that much that he is draped in diamonds?" As well, keep all bracelets and chains at home for your casual

or non–business functions. Chunky bracelets and chains often detract from a dark suit. Jewellery attracts the eye, and the more it shines or twinkles, the greater the tendency for the client to be distracted and lose focus on what you are saying. Finally, if you are a gentleman who has one or both ears pierced, remove your earring(s) before going to work. Many employers are uncomfortable with rings in gentlemen's ears. Save your earring(s) for non–business occasions.

6. **Do not bite your fingernails or cut them too short.** Keep your nails clean and short, but not too short. According to Barry Triller, Executive Vice President at Sun Life Canada, "When your nails are too short, people think you bite your nails — a tell–tale sign of nervousness or inability to control stress." Barry's trick is to keep approximately a 1mm band of white showing on his nails, such that each nail looks clean, short and well manicured. Many effective salespeople speak using their hands for emphasis. Naturally, the client's eye will be drawn to your hands and, unconsciously, they will evaluate your strength of character or lack thereof by the condition of your nails.
7. **Do not wear white gym socks under a suit.** Gym socks are not professional and should only be worn while exercising. Wearing them with casual pants or a suit is not appropriate. Wear clean, co–ordinating socks without holes.
8. **Never have tattoos or body/face piercings visible during business hours.** Tattoos and body piercings have become increasingly popular of late, especially with young adults. There was a time, not so long ago, that anyone who wore a tattoo marked themselves as being of lower socio–economic class, similar to someone who smoked cigarettes. Many business executives and salespeople would be wise to remember that they are on display all the time. Publicly displaying tattoos sends many messages, none of which are considered professional in

North American business arenas.

9. **Avoid flashy, ostentatious clothes and jewellery.** They not only detract from your role as a professional, they diminish your authority. John Lanni, the Assistant Vice–President of Training and Development for Clarica, an Insurance and Investment company which consists of 4000 advisors says, "When you are over–dressed, you are noticed. When you are under–dressed, you are noticed." The trick is to find the sweet spot where people don't say, "Look at the way he's dressed!" Never dress to the *lowest–common denominator*, and always remember, you are dressing for a role. Your attire, or costume, if you will, must always reflect your role.
10. **Hairstyles.** I interviewed Cecile Davis, Sole–Proprietor of Hairzona, a full–service Hair and Esthetics Business. Her advice to gentlemen in sales and executive professions is to keep your hair clean, short and well–groomed. She advises that hair should be well–trimmed and, although hair can be longer on the top of the head, great pains should be taken to ensure that hair around the ears and nape of the neck is kept short and not "scraggly." Cecile further advises that gentlemen should get their hair cut every three weeks. In between those hair cuts, the hair that tends to grow at the nape of the neck should be trimmed twice a week. "If you have a regular hair stylist, have them trim the nape of your neck a couple of times a week. Most hair stylists will perform this function free of charge," says Cecile. With regards to hair products, gentlemen may use gels and mousse to keep hair in place and give it some style, allowing one to exercise some individuality. Exercise caution and restraint as to how much product is used. Sometimes less is more. The customer should not be distracted by the Sales Professional's hair. A conservative, well–groomed look that is short around the collar is best. Cecile suggests that men with facial hair should keep

it well–trimmed and very short. Finally, if you are going to put highlights, lowlights or streaks in your hair, make sure they look very natural and that the application is minimal. Again, work towards achieving a look that is appropriate in your role as opposed to one that is flashy.

BUSINESS DRESS FOR WOMEN

1. **Always wear nylons or hose in the business environment.** Bare legs, no matter how warm it is outside are not professional. In the event that you are called to a client's home, removing your shoes at the front door, which is customary, will result in your toes being exposed. Not a good position for negotiating sales.
2. **Wear closed–toe and closed–back shoes.** Sandals are much too casual, even in the heat of the summer: they send a more relaxed, casual message, which diminishes your negotiating power.
3. **Pastel colours should seldom be worn during business interviews.** Always wear primary colours — for example, black and white, red and black, red and white, dark blue and white. Primary colours are high–powered and give you an added energy boost, particularly when you are tired.
4. **Always wear cosmetics.** Applied correctly and with a skilled–hand, cosmetics enhance the contours of your face, frame your lips and give depth to your eyes. Get into the habit of wearing cosmetics. Remember, the key to successful makeup application is that it is a skill, just like learning to drive a car. Certainly, you wouldn't drive a car without lessons, and the same applies to cosmetic application. Barbara Bond, Senior Sales Director at Mary Kay Cosmetics states, "I think that people totally underestimate the value of makeup. A particular technique that should be remembered during makeup application is that other people see you at arm's length, so you need to *hold the mirror at arm's length*. Makeup application starts with the eyes, then

moves to the lips and the cheeks, which should be balanced in between." Barbara suggests women purchase a larger mirror than just a hand-held one in order to get the bigger picture. The reason for the arm's length test is because of proxemics. In North America in particular, people don't generally invade your personal space. They tend to see you from an arm's length distance. Make sure you see what they see. Barbara, whose profession is built on teaching women to successfully enhance their image through professional makeup application, colours and techniques states, "I think that when women wear makeup, what they say to people is that they take care of themselves and will, therefore, take care of their customers. Usually, women don't wear makeup not because they don't want to wear makeup, but because they don't know how to wear it." Application techniques and colour suitability tests can be done through any Mary Kay Cosmetics consultant. I think that people totally underestimate the power of makeup. In a recent issue of *O*, Oprah Winfrey's magazine, a report by Christine Fellingham entitled, *What Your Makeup Says About You* clearly demonstrated how the right makeup can raise your salary. Fellingham writes that in one study conducted by Judith Waters, PhD, Professor of Psychology at Fairleigh Dickinson University, eight women were photographed in their own everyday makeup and then those same women were photographed after a professional makeup application. Either a "before" or "after" photo was attached to a resume presenting them as potential job candidates and taken to 500 corporate employment agencies and human resources executives. The resumes with photos in which the women were wearing professional makeup were all relegated to a salary range 20 percent higher. "The message was unmistakably clear," said Waters. "The results show that it pays to look good." Doe Lang, PhD, a psychotherapist and life coach in New York City and the author of *The New Secrets of Charisma,* explains that the most universally accepted makeup is the most natural–looking. "When it mimics a healthy, natural look, it makes you appear confident and happy because you're enhancing your own beauty; you're not trying to change or hide yourself." On the flip side, makeup that's applied with a clumsy hand sends an altogether different set of signals. Wearing too much makeup screams a lack of self–confidence. "A woman in heavy makeup is communicating that she's not comfortable in her own skin," says Waters. A lack of makeup and unwashed hair can be signs of depression," says Debbie Then, PhD, a Los Angeles Psychologist who focuses on self–esteem and image issues. This makes intuitive sense, as women who look good and feel good about themselves project a far more confident image.

5. **How tight is too tight?** Although fashion trends have changed in many different directions for casual clothing, professional clothing trends have changed very little. Tight blouses, tight skirts, tight pants, tight anything, doesn't hold up well in the professional environment. Due to the obvious facts that women have breasts and that tight blouses draw attention to them, wearing tight–fitting shirts or blouses distracts co–workers, clients, and everyone else for that matter. One male executive stated, "If it stops me in my tracks, it's inappropriate." Tight clothes draw the eye and shift the person's concentration from what is being said to them to what is in front of them. Body language is much louder than anything your mouth could be saying. If you wish people to see you as a professional, intelligent, capable woman, tight clothing should be kept away from the business environment. I am not suggesting that you wear clothing that is loose and baggy and looks as though you are wearing a potato sack. The best way to describe the look that is most professional is "tailored." A well–tailored outfit fits well and complements the

body shape as opposed to snugly fitting the body shape. The best test for checking whether an outfit is too tight is to ensure that there aren't any stress lines across the front or the back of the outfit, and that the undergarments you are wearing aren't visible through the outfit.

6. **How short is too short?** When it comes to the length of dresses and skirts in the fashion houses of haute couture, styles have come and gone over the years. Interestingly, hemlines in the business world have not undergone the same drastic changes. Professional women should ensure that their hemlines aren't higher than 1.5 inches above the top of the knee. There are two reasons for this. Sitting becomes awkward if your skirt is too short. Skirts automatically rise up when one sits, vastly increasing the amount of leg that is visible, thus distracting from what you are saying. The second reason has more to do with the role you are trying to fill. Be mindful that the role of efficient, competent, intelligent Sales Executive or Sales Professional does not blend well with the sexy–legged, Tina Turner look.
7. **Cleavage — what exactly are you selling?** With the advent of "dress down" Fridays and Business Casual attire employers are contending with the problem of cleavage much more than ever before. Low–cut, revealing blouses, tank tops, or t–shirts send mixed messages and very much detract from the professional appearance that is required of the role of a salesperson or Sales Executive. My advice on this front (pardon the pun) is to save the cleavage and "hootchie tops" for the bars. One other very important piece of advice — always wear a bra unless you are going to bed. Wearing a bra improves your posture and keeps everything where it should be, if you get my meaning.
8. **Hairstyles.** Cecile Davis advises women to remember "there is no such thing as wash and go hair." All hair should be blow–dried and styled using products like gel and mousse to ensure

that the shape of the style is retained throughout the day. I can't stress enough how important it is that women get into the habit of doing their hair *every morning* before leaving the house. Clean, well-styled and neatly groomed hair gives the appearance of confidence and happiness. In fact, psychotherapists can usually tell when a woman is suffering from prolonged periods of depression by taking note of unclean, un-styled hair for days on end. In addition, women who have well-styled, well-groomed hair tend to flick their hair less, an unconscious gesture used by many women to take the hair off their face — and a very distracting one at that. Invest in a good haircut. Speak to your stylist about the type of work you do and the image you are trying to portray. The stylist can then advise you on which style is most suitable given your role as a Sales Professional. Many women make the mistake of waiting too long to cut their hair. Depending on the length, style, and rate of growth of your hair, most hair professionals suggest that you wait no longer than six to eight weeks between trims. Keep highlights, lowlights and colours looking as natural as possible. If you colour your hair to cover grey, ensure that you continue to re-apply the colour every three to four weeks to ensure that the grey doesn't peek through as your hair grows. Colour, contrast and texture are essential elements of hair design. Ensure that your hair reflects your special personality.

9. **Avoid flashy, ostentatious jewellery. Jewellery should be kept to a minimum.** With Professional Saleswomen and Executive women in general, the rule with jewellery is *less is more.* Dangly bracelets and earrings are distracting. You never want your client focusing on the dangle of your earrings or the glitter of your bracelets while you are giving your sales presentation. Wear one chain, not three. Wear one or two rings, preferably a gold band, not six. Earrings should complement your

outfit, but should preferably be silver or gold studs or small rings which don't dangle. Keep earrings to just one earring per ear, and remove the additional rings that surround the upper cartilage of the ear during business hours.

10. **Never have body/face piercings visible during business hours.** Although tattoos and body piercings are enjoying a great deal of popularity, especially among young adults, the same enthusiasm for piercings and tattoos has not permeated the business world. Women are judged quite harshly and in not too flattering terms when they expose tattoos or piercings in the business world. Up until quite recently, and this might still be the case with many people, someone sporting a tattoo was considered to hail from a lower socio–economic background. As such, they weren't likely to be promoted as quickly as a non-tattooed colleague. Rightly or wrongly, tattoos give people the impression that the wearer comes from an uneducated and poor background, and this does impact your chances of promotion and advancement in the business world. As one business executive stated, "Executives and salespeople are on display all the time and the way they look reflects their commitment to the role and its importance in the organization." Although employers are unlikely to mention your tattoos or piercings directly to you, they often find them to be in "bad taste" and reflect a "lack of commitment to the role."

Robert Ezra Park, the noted researcher and author, once wrote: "It is probably no mere accident that the word *person*, in its first meaning, is a mask. It is rather a recognition of the fact that everyone is always and everywhere, more or less consciously, playing a role… It is in these roles that we know each other; it is in these roles that we know ourselves."

Our style of dress impacts not only how others see us and react to us, it impacts how we see ourselves. If you see yourself as a Sales Professional whose products and services enhance the quality of the customers you serve, then you will find yourself dressing in that fashion. If, however, you perceive yourself as a "junk peddler," you don't much care for the people you serve or your product, and you are just selling to pay the rent, that too will come out in the way you present yourself.

Energy Enhancing Colours

Dark red, burgundy, maroon, orange, turquoise, mustard yellow, royal purple — Wearing these colours when you are tired will help perk you up and make you look less tired. Save these colours for the morning after a restless night or a night with insufficient hours of sleep as any one of these colours will "bring you to life."

Powerful Colours

Black, dark blue, bold red, dark grey — These colours convey passion, integrity, authority, confidence and will hold people's attention.

When a Sales Professional chooses his or her attire any given morning, they should "dress to impress." Much can be said of the salesperson wearing a well-ironed shirt with crisp trousers as opposed to one that is wearing a well-worn, crushed shirt with coffee stains down the front. Benjamin Franklin once said, "Well done is better than well said." Take the time to look professional and you will impress your client without having to say too much.

CHAPTER 2
BEHAVIOUR MODIFICATION EXERCISES

1. Spend a day identifying the number of people you meet who are wearing a uniform (*e.g.* police officer, business person, student, rebel, housewife, athlete, doctor, minister, nurse, *etc.*). What messages do the uniforms convey about their roles and the expected sets of behaviours attached to their roles?
2. Compare and contrast people's reactions to you depending on your attire. How do they respond to you when you are casually dressed versus when you are dressed for business? Is there a difference in their body language? Is there a difference in yours?
3. Spend one hour cleaning and buffing your shoes.
4. Cull your wardrobe of clothing. Remove clothing that you haven't worn for two or more years.
5. Purchase a quality, non–stick steam iron and "crisp up your clothes" before wearing them.
6. Segment your wardrobe and co–ordinate three or four high–power outfits to wear in a business situation.

CHAPTER 3:

Paralanguage

Simply put, paralanguage deals with *how* something is said, and not *what* is said. The term *paralanguage* refers to other vocal cues people use to communicate, as opposed to the explicit words that are used. For example, loudness of voice, pauses, silences, hesitations, rate, inflections, and the like all fall into the category of paralanguage.

Paralanguage, if used to its full effect, can communicate a vast array of messages. A skilled Sales Professional learns to use paralanguage to his/her best advantage. Many companies spend hundreds of thousands of dollars to ensure their salespeople can communicate the features, advantages and benefits of their product lines. Unfortunately, a scant 7% of what is said during a sales interview is retained by clients. A resoundingly high 38% of communication is based not on the actual words themselves but on how the words are delivered. Interesting, isn't it? We spend so much time, money and energy on learning to say the exact words because words are the key that unlock the mind. Yet, we spend next to no time on how to deliver the words with the passion, energy and enthusiasm that is essential to unlocking the heart.

Rule #3:

You can open people's minds using words, but your voice is the key that unlocks their heart.

A highly skilled non–verbal communicator spends a great deal of time learning how to deliver a sales presentation using tone, loudness, pauses, inflection and the like to increase the effectiveness of his/her words and make them more memorable. Very simply, it isn't just what you say, but how you say it that makes communicating with others powerful.

Truly powerful, successful salespeople have learned the importance of delivery. They have learned the important effect projecting their voice, pausing, and using planned silences has on their presentations, especially in terms of captivating their audiences and projecting an aura of confidence and enthusiasm.

Correct use of tone, inflection and pauses not only increases your customer's attention and interest in what you are saying, it increases the perception that you have a greater knowledge of your product, its features and its benefits.

The various qualities of a speaker's voice provide information about the speaker. Studies show that people make assumptions about intelligence, friendliness, social status, general attitudes and honesty based on paralanguage, or *how a speaker sounds.*

TONE AND LOUDNESS OF VOICE

"A really powerful, interesting and arresting voice is one that has a bottom to it."

— Dwight Powell, Regional Vice–President, Clarica

Have you ever watched a television evangelist preach? Evangelical preachers have the power to enthral their audiences. Their charisma, passion, energy and their *voice* reach out and touch the people to whom they speak. Whether their audience is right in front of them or thousands of miles away in a living room, these speakers know that anyone who has tuned in especially to hear their message must be touched by both the message *and the unshakable delivery* of the message.

Evangelical speakers have the gift of being able to lend passion to their words. They have the gift of lifting the words from their script and throwing them to all four corners of the room. Their message resonates. They aren't just reading from a script. In fact, they rarely consult their script, they know it so well. They go one step further from just knowing their script. They *own* their script.

To own your script so that your message seems effortless you have to PRACTICE HOW YOU PREACH, NOT JUST WHAT YOU PREACH.

There are *two* skill–sets you need in order to achieve a deep, rich, baritone voice which holds people spellbound.

1. **Know your content.** Know your product, its functions, benefits, features and all the bells and whistles that accompany it backwards, forwards, inside and out. Your ability to deliver your sales presentation will only be heightened by over–learning your product. No amount of fine delivery will hide your lack of knowledge about what you sell. There is no short–cut to this. Know your product.
2. **Develop low frequencies in your voice.** A low–frequency voice is one with a low pitch. The pitch — how high or low the sound — is chiefly determined by the frequency. The higher the frequency (the more vibrations per second), the higher the sound. The lower the frequency (the fewer vibrations per second), the

lower the sound. Simply put, it is easier to listen to someone whose frequency does not have as many vibrations. The sound is more pleasing to the ear, particularly as we grow older. When you hear the voices of well-known news anchors like Lloyd Robertson and Peter Mansbridge and other television personalities like Oprah Winfrey and Barbara Walters, Dan Rather and the legendary Walter Cronkite, to name a few, their voices have more bass, are lower-frequency, and resonate with authority and confidence. A voice with a lot of bass in it resonates further into the room without the assistance of a microphone. The best way to develop a low-frequency voice, according to Powell, is to "speak from your belly and your diaphragm rather than the back of your throat." A low-frequency voice has "a bottom to it." Many radio broadcasters have this quality of low frequency to their voice. Their voices, rather than being high-pitched and squeaky, come across as low. If you already have a low voice, you have a great advantage. Men's voices are seldom high-pitched. Most men have a low-frequency, low-pitched quality to the timbre of their voices especially after puberty. Women, on the other hand, have been traditionally socialized to develop a soft, high-frequency pitch to their voices as a measure of their femininity. As such, their high-pitched voices lack the bass necessary for their words to resonate across the room without sounding as though they are screaming. Powell's advice to women in particular is to "practice howling and yelling" in an empty room while deliberately dropping the pitch of your voice lower than you are accustomed to hearing it. Practice speaking using lower tones at least three times a week and take professional coaching if necessary. Your voice is a very important component of your communicating abilities. Keep honing it until "it's got a bottom to it."

PAUSES AND HESITATIONS

Pauses, short unfilled silences, are powerful tools in speech, often conveying strong messages, especially in sales presentations. Pauses convey a myriad of different messages, some good and some bad. When pauses are used too frequently in a conversation, the listener perceives the speaker as contemptuous, angry or anxious. Excessive pausing by the salesperson may also indicate a lack of preparedness or understanding of the features of the product. On the other hand, used properly, pauses increase the degree to which the speaker is perceived as concise and precise. It also adds a dimension of unpredictability to a conversation, making the speaker's responses appear more intelligent and considered. The trick to pausing at correct times is to follow these specific guidelines:

1. Pause after asking a question, and don't interrupt with a response until your prospect has had the opportunity to answer.
2. Pause after making an emotional point, thus allowing your prospect the opportunity to absorb the impact of the emotion.
3. Pause after making a humorous statement, allowing the client to understand the humour and respond accordingly.
4. Pause frequently when selling to ethnically diverse clients who are still mastering the intricacies of the English language. Pauses afford them the opportunity to translate some of your words and understand you.
5. Pause before you respond to heated questions from your clients. Let them see that you are gathering your thoughts before you answer and are giving their points serious consideration.
6. Give your client options, then pause and wait for an answer.

The legendary sales trainer, J. Douglas Edwards stressed the importance of silence after asking a "closing question." He said, "Whenever you ask a closing question, you shut up! Whoever talks first 'loses'!"

There is nothing as powerful in the sales process as well–planned silence.

In North America, we use pauses a great deal in our conversations. The trouble is that many of our pauses are *filled pauses*. Filled pauses are hesitations and pauses that the speaker fills with various non–word vocalizations. In English these commonly include such sounds as "um," "uh," "er," "ah," "eh." Filled pauses also include word repetition or false starts, stuttering, and verbal expressions acting as fillers (such as "OK" or " like, you know" or "anyway" when used out of context).

Filled pauses are very irritating to listen to for prolonged periods of time. They detract from everything the speaker is saying. When a speaker uses a great number of filled pauses, they sound hesitant, unsure, anxious, nervous and doubtful. Filled pauses demonstrate indecision and a lack of confidence. The trouble with filled pauses is that speakers who use them in their conversations routinely form the habit of using "um," "uh," "er," "ah," "eh," "like, you know," "anyway," in all their conversations. Like breathing or blinking, they do it unconsciously, and when they hear their tape–recorded voices, many are shocked to hear how many filled pauses dominate and detract from their conversation. This is why it is so important to record and then listen to yourself on tape. It allows you to hear what others hear.

Ridding yourself of the habit of using "um," "uh," "er," "ah," in conversation is as difficult as ridding yourself of the habit of smoking. A habit that is acquired over a period of years won't disappear overnight. It takes the same amount of persistence, tenacity, effort and determination to rid yourself of filled pauses as it does to stop smoking. Here are a few suggestions:

1. On tape, describe the benefits and features of your product offerings. Now, listen to the tape. How many filled pauses do you

notice?

2. Write out a description of the benefits and features of your product. Read it on tape. Listen to the tape. Take note of the reduction in the "ums" and "uhs."
3. Use shorter sentences. Usually "ums" and "uhs" are used to bridge thoughts. Keep your thoughts and your sentences concise.
4. Speak into a tape recorder at least three times a week. Listen to the recording. Take note of the number of filled pauses. When did they occur? At what point in the speech? Are you more nervous starting out or do you get restless towards the end? Are the filled pauses more pronounced at the beginning of the speech or at the end?
5. Repeat the exercise three or four times a week and you *will* see a marked improvement in the reduction of filled pauses by the end of the second week.

The key to reducing the hesitations and filled pauses in your speech is to be keenly aware of the fact that you do use them, how often you use them and understand that they detract from the power of your words. No matter how well you know your subject matter, no matter how well you are dressed, no matter what you are selling, if you use too many hesitations and filled pauses your closing rate will be low.

Your customers aren't just buying your product. They are buying you. People buy, not because they understand, but because your verbal, non–verbal and paralanguages line up to convince them that you understand and believe your product or service will help them.

They are buying because of your confidence, your energy, your enthusiasm. Let your voice, your tone, your presentation command people to action. Your voice is capable of leading people to take action NOW.

SILENCE

"I am afraid of your silence because of what it could mean. I suspect your silence of meaning you are getting bored or losing interest or making up your own mind about me without my guidance. I believe that as long as I keep you talking I can know what you are thinking. But silence can also mean confidence. And mutual respect. Silence can mean live and let live: the appreciation that I am I and you are you. The silence is an affirmation that we are already together — as two people. Words can mean that I want to make you into a friend and silence can mean that I accept your already being one."

— Hugh Prather

Silence is also a very powerful non–verbal communication tool. There is an old joke that says, "It is better to keep silent and to have people think you are a fool than to speak and remove all doubt." Successful Sales Professionals use silence routinely to enhance the impact and intensity of what they say.

Do you remember Rule #1? SELLING ISN'T TELLING. Silence says more than words in many cases. In his book *Etcetera*, J. Vernon Jensen suggests that a wide range of meanings are attributable to silence. He suggests that silence indicates:

1. mental activity, such as reflection or thoughtfulness
2. evaluation and passing judgement
3. revelation, for example, hiding a fact or making a fact known by answering an inquiry with silence
4. emotional expression, generally of strong emotions, such as love or disgust; and
5. an accent or underscoring of a point.

Silence is a language unto itself. As Jensen suggests, silence may indicate that you are carefully considering a point before passing judgement. People perceive you as being thoughtful and careful in your evaluations. People judge you to be filled with insight and intelligence as a result. Silence also conveys disgust, anger, disagreement and many other strong emotions without using words. Words are irretrievable and can do untold harm. Silence doesn't do as much damage because it is left to the interpretation of the listener.

Attentive Silence

There is great value in allowing your customer the freedom to think, feel and express himself. "The beginning of wisdom is silence," said a Hebrew sage. "The second stage is listening."

Most "listeners" talk too much. They may speak as much or even more than the person trying to talk. Learning the art of silent responsiveness is essential to good listening. After all, another person cannot describe a problem if you are doing all the talking.

Silence on the part of the listener gives the speaker time to think about what he is going to say and thus enables him to go deeper into himself. It gives a person space to experience the feelings churning within. Silence also allows the speaker to proceed at his own pace. It provides time to deal with his ambivalence about the buying decision. Silence often serves as a gentle nudge to go further into a conversation. When a sales interview is studded with significant silences and backed by good listening and attending, the results can be very impressive.

People are generally uncomfortable with silence. Even a few seconds' pause in the conversation causes many people to squirm in discomfort. People feel so ill at ease with silence that they have a strong inner compulsion to alleviate their discomfort by ending the silence. For these people, the focus of attention is not on the speaker but on their own inner disquiet.

Fortunately, most people can increase their comfort with silence in a relatively short period of time. When people find out what to do in silence, they become far less uptight in the verbal lulls that are so important to vital communication. During the pauses in an interaction, a good listener does the following:

1. **Attends to the speaker.** Her body posture demonstrates that she is really there for the other person, usually leaning a bit forward and directing her body towards the speaker.
2. **Observes the speaker.** She understands that the speaker's eyes, facial expressions, posture, and gestures are all communicating something. When you observe your speaker's body language, you can also "hear" what your speaker isn't saying.
3. **Thinks about what the speaker is communicating.** She ponders what the speaker has just said and how the speaker might be feeling. She considers a variety of responses and selects the one which she belives will be most effective.

Listening is a combination of hearing what another person is saying and involvement with the person who is speaking. Your clients will appreciate the time you take to actively listen to them. Many Sales Professionals make the mistake of talking too much and listening not at all. The cliché is that we were given two ears and one mouth. In a selling situation, we should use them in that proportion. Avoid interrupting your client while she is speaking. Listen not only with your ears, but with your whole body. One particular example of this is *nodding.* Nodding serves three purposes:

1. It communicates that you are actively paying attention.
2. It encourages the speaker to continue in their line of thought.
3. It respects and acknowledges their statements.

Let your client know that you are actively listening to all that they say and do not say. Listening is a crucial form of body language. The great sales and motivational speakers Jack and Garry Kinder of Dallas, Texas, say that true Sales Professionals listen with three ears:

1. One ear that hears what people say.
2. Another ear that hears what they don't say.
3. The third, and most important ear, listens for what they might *want* to say but don't know how to say.

CHAPTER 3
BEHAVIOUR MODIFICATION EXERCISES

1. Tape–record your opening statement of product benefits. Listen to it and then deliberately, in an exaggerated fashion, re–record yourself, lower your resonance using the principles from this chapter. Repeat and practise daily.
2. Watch this evening's newscast and tape your version of the lead story. Listen to it. Do you hear a believable and authoritative voice?
3. Phone a friend this evening. Make a conscious attempt to reduce the number of non–filled pauses in your conversation.

CHAPTER 4:

Eye Contact

One Saturday afternoon, my husband Jack and I were rushing from our home in Waterloo to get to the Tilley Endurables store in downtown Toronto before it closed. Driving an hour and a half to a retail store would generally qualify you as a "motivated buyer." Jack, who heads up a sales force of 4000 people, had just agreed to the purchase of one hat for each member of the sales force (a retail value of approximately $200,000). That's a lot of hats!

He may well have been the biggest customer to have ever walked through the front door of the store. But like all customers, he did not arrive with a neon sign over his head announcing either past, potential present or future sales opportunities.

The reason we were rushing to the store that day had to do with Jack's upcoming trip to Amsterdam. Tilley is famous for its travel and leisure wear, and since Jack had just done business with the company, he was aware of their product line. Having perused their catalogue, Jack decided to purchase a few choice articles for his trip.

Tilley's downtown Toronto location is in the very posh, very beautiful Queen's Quay Terminal. We got there at 4 p.m., hoping the store hadn't already closed, hurriedly paid the parking attendant $15 and raced through the terminal to get to the store. Breathing a collective sigh of relief upon learning that the store didn't close until 6 p.m., we proceeded, at a more leisurely pace, to find the clothing Jack was specifically looking for.

Jack's first attempt at getting the salesperson's assistance was met with her, literally, turning her body towards another section of the counter so that she could continue to fold articles of clothing. She wasn't serving anyone at the time. He politely asked her where the men's clothing was. She looked up with what can only be described as a "disinterested" gaze and pointed towards one wall. She didn't look at Jack, nor did she look at me. She opted, instead, to continue folding. There was another salesperson at the service desk as well. The two women continued a private conversation they were having when we initially walked into the store and treated us like we were not there.

Jack and I were a little annoyed at this obvious inattention, but since we had driven an hour and a half to get here and paid $15 to park, we decided to persist. Jack was in the market for two pairs of wrinkle-resistant travel trousers (with the hidden, pickpocket-proof pockets), some matching shirts, and some undergarments. After about five minutes of searching through an array of possibilities, Jack had specific questions about the different products on display and their suitability for his particular travel needs. Jack went to the service desk a second time and asked his question. Neither woman looked up. I continued to search for his sizes and try to decide on which pants would be most suitable. He came back looking more than a little frustrated. We continued our search but, by this time, we really did need help.

Jack walked up to the desk a third time and asked, "Do you have any salespeople here?" The woman behind the counter barely looked up, very annoyed at being disrupted from her folding and talking and said, "We don't believe in salespeople."

We left.

That woman had no idea that she was speaking to someone who had just bought $200,000 worth of Tilley hats. She didn't even take the trouble to look up at him. Eye contact is an essential opening step in connecting and welcoming every potential buyer. Every buyer should be valued, not just for their potential current transaction, but also, for all past and future transactions, as well as the business they might influence. This is why well–managed hotel chains have created programs to identify their most loyal customers. They want to know things like how often you have stayed with them in the past, what company you are affiliated with, what rate category you fall under, and what amenities and special services they should be extending to you.

If the Tilley employee had stopped her conversation and her folding for just one minute, she would have learned that we had spent over an hour driving to the store and, psychologically, were there to buy. She would also have understood that to say, "We don't believe in salespeople" to someone who is a salesperson, or who leads salespeople, or who is related to a salesperson, is a *direct insult.* Would she have said, "We don't believe in teachers" and thereby alienate all teachers and people who respect teachers?

The Tilley product line is positioned as high value. We had fully expected to spend approximately $1000 for a couple of pairs of pants, some shirts and related products. This experience is an excellent example of the fact that, regardless of the quality of the product, the merchandising, the advertising, the store locations, pricing, displays, *etc.*, it all comes down to the salesperson at the point of sale. A thoughtless or ineffective salesperson can destroy all the other components in the value chain of a product offering.

It was quite evident from the way the employees in that store conducted themselves that they didn't consider themselves salespeople. They do not deserve that distinction.

Sales Professionals take pride in their work. They understand that knowledge of their products, their understanding of the features, advantages and benefits of what they sell, and their knowledge of their customer's needs make them invaluable assets to their clients, specifically, and to the economy in general. Sales Professionals also understand the psychology of selling and the body language that underlies this psychology.

If either of the women behind the counter at Tilley had taken a moment to look at Jack, they would have seen many things. One look into his eyes would have revealed how excited he was about his upcoming trip to Amsterdam. Had either one taken the time to ask him where he was going, or where he had come from, they would have realized that no one drives an hour and a half and pays $15 for parking four days before their trip *just to browse.* Jack could have been sold with very little effort.

The greatest damage done, by far, was to both the reputation of Tilley and that of Sales Professionals in general.

After we left the downtown location, I persuaded Jack to drive to the Don Mills store, which was much bigger and, as it turned out, where the sales force was excellent. The gentleman who served us was courteous, made meaningful eye contact and did an excellent job detailing the different product offerings. Unfortunately, by this time Jack was soured on the whole deal. Even though he tried on several items, some of which were fabulous, he left without purchasing anything. His initial encounter at the downtown store left him soured and with his mind made up. His rationalization was that he could buy the equivalent clothing for a fraction of the cost at any number of high volume retailers. The second salesperson, although he did an excellent job, could not undo the damage done by the first. He could not, despite his best efforts, make *the sale before the sale.*

If I had to choose the single, most serious error in this incident, it would be the failure of these women to establish immediate eye contact. Eye contact has long been recognized as a means of communicating without speaking. Effective eye contact expresses interest and a desire to listen. It involves focusing one's eyes softly on the speaker and occasionally shifting the gaze from his face to other parts of the body, to a gesturing hand, for example, then back to the face and then to eye contact once again.

Poor eye contact occurs when a listener repeatedly looks away from the speaker, stares at him constantly or blankly, or looks away as soon as the speaker looks at the listener.

Eye contact enables the speaker to appraise your receptiveness to him and his message. It helps him figure out how safe he is with you. Equally important, you can "hear" the speaker's deeper meanings through eye contact. Indeed, if effective listening means getting inside the other's skin and understanding the person's experience from his perspective (establishing empathy), one of the best ways to enter that inner world is through the "window" of the eyes.

Ralph Waldo Emerson said, "The eyes of men converse as much as their tongues, but with the advantage that the ocular dialect needs no dictionary, but is understood the world over."

Emerson was right. In a multi–cultural world where so many cultures blend together daily and our customers are from many parts of the world, it is hard to know which behaviours are appropriate and which may be construed as offensive. Thankfully, this is not the case with eye contact. The ocular dialect needs no dictionary and it is a dialect that is understood by all. While we are speaking to someone, establishing eye contact conveys respect for that person, interest in that person and a general attraction to that person.

In order for Sales Professionals to build relationships with their clients and enhance customer loyalty, it is essential for them to build empathy. The dictionary defines empathy as the power of understanding and imaginatively entering into and understanding another's feelings. What better method of starting to build empathy than by appropriate eye contact?

Many people have a difficult time establishing and maintaining eye contact. Just as some people have a hard time knowing what to do with their hands in social situations, other people do not know what to do with their eyes. The importance of eye contact can not be overemphasized. People measure the truth of what you are saying by your ability to meet and hold their gaze. In fact, people who experience difficulty maintaining eye contact are described as "shifty," "dishonest," "untrustworthy," "shy," "unassertive," "sneaky" and the list goes on. These aren't qualities Professional Salespeople would want attached to them.

Despite the fact that some people find it difficult to look into another's eyes, few of us enjoy carrying on a conversation with a person whose glance continually darts about the room. When I am listened to by that kind of person, I am distracted from what I am saying. For example, when a person talking with me at a party keeps looking around the room at other people, I often interpret that to mean that he would rather be someplace else — and I personally wish he would find out where he would rather be and go there! Lack of eye contact may be a sign of indifference or hostility. It can be experienced as a put–down.

Eye contact also speaks to the issue of status and dominance. Traditionally, those members of society who were of lower socio–economic status were not allowed to meet the gaze of their richer, higher socio–economic counterparts. Therefore, anyone who was so bold as to meet the gaze of nobility must also be nobility. Professional salespeople understand their value and have respect for their work, especially those professionals who are successful. In meeting the gaze of their clients, what they are saying is:

1. Yes, I can be trusted.
2. Yes, I like and respect you and will do everything in my power to assist you in your needs.
3. Yes, I am confident in who I am and in the integrity of my products.

When Ralph Waldo Emerson said, "the eyes of men converse as much as their tongues," what he didn't mention is that our eyes tell the truth, the whole truth, and nothing but the truth. In fact, we have no control over the dilation and contraction of our pupils; the motion is a reflex, completely automatic. The science of neurolinguistic programming is devoted, in large measure, to the unconscious movement of eyes as people access their memories, emotions or imaginings.

For example, our pupils respond to emotions as well as to light. When we look at someone or something highly desirable, our pupils dilate as if to take in more of the view. Pupils also dilate when we are frightened, telling a lie or sexually aroused. Our pupil size is also related to mental effort — the more intense the mental activity, the larger our pupils become. As you can see, our eyes are far more than passive instruments in our heads, taking in visual images. Our eyes are very important and strong communication tools.

The ability to have good eye contact is essential for effective interpersonal communication in our society. It is one of the most effective of the listening skills. Use your eyes to command attention, to captivate your customer and to enhance the potency of your words. Use your eyes to convey interest in your prospect. Touch people with your eyes.

Let your customer know that you are interested and that they are interesting!

One Saturday evening, around 8 p.m., my husband and I decided to go out for dinner. We both dressed up — he wore a jacket and mock turtleneck sweater with dress pants and I wore an ankle–length sweater dress. We got to the restaurant at 8:30 p.m. and were relieved to see there were seven empty tables. It's a small neighbourhood restaurant and wasn't busy as many of the regular dinner patrons had already left. We were the only people standing by the front. We waited for five minutes before a waiter even noticed us. And when he did notice us, he said, "We are *really* busy, just wait there while I get you a table." For the next ten minutes, he assiduously avoided eye contact with us. Keep in mind there were seven empty tables where we might have been seated. He kept his back to us, spoke to people at great length at a table of six and diligently avoided all eye contact with us. After waiting for nearly twenty minutes, without the slightest attention or service from him, we left. At this point I didn't care how good their chocolate–banana cake was.

The moral of this event and all commercial transactions — *Business goes where it is wanted and stays where it is serviced.*

CHAPTER 4
BEHAVIOUR MODIFICATION EXERCISES

1. Spend a day deliberately focusing on increasing eye contact with everyone you meet. Ensure that you don't stare just above their heads, or at their foreheads or noses.
2. Track the number of people you meet who glance away while speaking to you. What messages are you getting? How do you feel?
3. Today, whenever you say "Hi" or "How are you?" to someone, hold eye contact for two to four seconds. Do you notice a difference in people's reactions to you?

CHAPTER 5:

Proxemics

"Don't stand...don't stand so...
Don't stand so close to me..."
— Sting

The way in which people use space communicates an important non–verbal message. How people use space in this way is called *proxemics.* Simply put, proxemics refers to perception and use of personal and interpersonal space.

The use of space has a powerful effect on communication. As Edward Hall, in his seminal work *The Hidden Dimension* has observed, *"Spatial changes give a tone to communication, accent it, and at times even override the spoken word."* If a person moves to a point that we believe is too close, we back up. Conversely, we tend to move closer to a person we believe to be too distant. How close is too close, and how far is too far, however, are carefully prescribed. Although the actual distance involved varies from culture to culture, the categorization of personal space according to appropriate and inappropriate distances when speaking is universal.

Hall identified four categories of personal space:

1. **Intimate** — from contact to 18 inches

2. **Casual–Personal** — from 1.5 feet to 4 feet
3. **Social–Consultative** — from 4 to 12 feet
4. **Public (lectures and speeches)** — greater than 12 feet.

The proper observances of these distances are crucial in North America, particularly in the sales and business arenas. Social–consultative personal space is the space employed in conducting most day–to–day affairs. It is the space in which business is conducted and is impersonal enough for use with strangers. Hall's work was published in 1966 but his range of 4 to 12 feet, which was what was recommended for Social–Consultative, or Sales functions, have still remained remarkably unchanged.

A common complaint by the public is that salespeople are "pushy." It is my perception that this term has more to do with body language than it does the content of the sales presentation. When people perceive that someone is violating their personal space, they perceive that person as being "pushy." The difficulty for Sales Professionals is that the more enthusiastically they describe their product and the more they gesticulate using their hands and arms, the greater the likelihood that they will violate the personal space of their customer. This is the chief reason that Sales Professionals should take great care to ensure that they respect the interpersonal space of their customer and maintain a 4 foot distance around the body of their client.

That said, many factors influence our proximity to others:

1. **Culture and ethnicity** — different cultures dictate different distances in personal space. For South Americans, Africans, Jamaicans and other people of Caribbean descent, Indonesians, Arabs, and French, conversing with a person dictates a much closer stance than normally comfortable for North Americans.
2. **Personal and physical traits** — age, height, weight and

certain physical attributes (*e.g.* physical disabilities and disfigurations). When conversing with someone shorter than you, stand further back so that they can see your face and eyes without having to strain their necks. When conversing with someone in a wheelchair, get a chair for yourself so that you can see each other at eye level.

3. **Interaction setting** — the context of the encounter — which affects both our willingness and expectations for distance. For example, when we are seated in a crowded bus or subway, we expect to have people both sitting and standing close to us, and we see nothing awkward about the situation.
4. **Perceived power or status** — greater distance is always given to those to whom we attribute, or who are vested with, power or status. Those with greater status, prestige, and power may occupy more space. For example, the CEO of a company usually has a large, corner office. Wealthy people in society usually have larger homes and vehicles. They are accustomed to having a great deal of space around them. Contrast that with the poor, socio–economically under–privileged people of low status who live in crowded buildings and crowded surroundings.
5. **The nature of the relationship** — whether we are interacting with friends, casual acquaintances, total strangers, coworkers, family members or romantic partners. We tend to move closer to people we like or feel interpersonal attraction for.
6. **The nature of the topic** — the extent to which a topic being discussed is confidential, highly personal and/or sensitive, or neutral.
7. **Gender roles** — although there are many contradictory findings regarding gender and interaction distance, the majority of researchers still find that women approach and are approached more closely by both genders.
8. **Personality traits** — the willingness to approach and to be

approached more closely by others is reflective of one's self-concept. People who are extroverts gain energy from the people around them. The more the merrier. They aren't usually bothered by someone entering into their personal zone. Introverts, however, guard their space and would prefer that others respect their boundaries.

It is important to keep in mind that although all eight of these factors influence distance, they are culturally determined. Moreover, even within the same culture there are variations in how "comfortable" we feel with our proxemic distance in our interaction with others. When others exceed our "comfort zone," this behaviour may be viewed as a "violation" of our space. Such intrusions, regardless of the intention, may be a potential source of conflict.

Customers can misinterpret a Sales Professional's closeness as inappropriately intimate, a sign of pushiness or even aggressiveness. Therefore, the need to be mindful of proxemics, especially when meeting someone for the first time, is of extreme value.

A good rule of thumb is that if your prospect backs up or leans back while you are speaking to him or her, you are likely violating their sense of space. This is a primal and unconscious dimension of non–verbal communication. If you doubt the importance of proxemics, try approaching a strange dog and watch its reaction as you approach its territory.

When I was interviewing people for this book, one interview, in particular, stands out in my mind. The gentleman I was interviewing is a successful businessman, and is extremely well–regarded and respected in his industry. He is in his mid–to–late 50s. When I walked into his office, he was standing behind his desk and asked me to be seated in a chair that was at least three feet back from his desk. There was a distance of approximately six feet between us. Two things struck me at the time. First, I felt that I was much further away from him than I would have liked to be. Secondly, when I asked him if I should keep my chair there or move it closer to the desk, he said it would be fine for me to be seated exactly where I was.

There was absolutely no tension in this interchange, and neither of us was the least bit embarrassed. However, I learned a very important rule of conduct regarding proximity as a result of this interaction. The salesperson should always take the cue from their customer with regards to proxemics. If your customer prefers to speak with less distance between you and you don't feel like your personal space is being violated, let that be your guide. Move yourself, or your chair closer to them keeping, at a minimum, three of your shoe lengths between you. If your customer moves closer, and you feel that they are literally "in your face," gently touch their left elbow with your right hand and while in the midst of conversation, take an imperceptible step backwards. This way, your client will not perceive you as being "haughty" or "superior" or "lacking in interest" or "aloof" or "cold" or "lacking in a desire to communicate" or any number of things that can go through their minds if you deliberately and obviously step back from them when they move forward.

This has got to be the most difficult of tasks. Measuring how close is too close and how far is too far is quite an individual characteristic. The distance between yourself and another person that most facilitates communication can be discovered by watching for signs of anxiety and discomfort in your client and then positioning yourself accordingly. Your challenge is to *match* or to *mimic* your client's proxemics and do so without violating your personal integrity. There are several ways you can do this, starting with the way you place your furniture in your office.

PLACEMENT OF OFFICE FURNITURE

The important thing to remember about placement of office furniture, especially if you regularly meet with a lot of people in your office, is flexibility. It is best to place the furniture in such a way as to deal with all manner of conversations and business/social interactions. Here are some guidelines for placement of office furniture:

1. **Don't have your back to the door of your office.** Have your chair facing the door and your desk directly in front of your chair. When someone comes into your office, stand up from your desk and move towards them, shake their hand, direct them as to where you would like them to sit, and then move back to your desk. Seeing someone's back immediately upon entering the office gives the visitor the feeling that they aren't welcome. If it isn't possible to directly face the door, at least have a peripheral sightline towards the door. This ensures two things: firstly, people aren't seeing your back as they enter, and secondly, it allows you the benefit of not being startled when people visit your office.
2. **Keep two client chairs in front of your desk.** There are times when it is necessary and beneficial to have a desk between yourself and your client. This is particularly the case during business meetings when both you and your client or prospect are taking notes or jotting down important discussion points. On the occasions when you wish to appear more authoritative, sitting behind a desk increases your power and status. Remember, when a person sits across from you at your desk, the nature of the interaction is more likely to be *role–to–role* (for example, employer to employee; salesperson to client or prospect) rather than *person–to–person* (for example, Gregory and Michael). Certainly, in the business environment, there is a need for role–to–role interaction. However, if you want a more relaxed, casual conversation, keep your client chair beside the desk rather than across the desk.
3. **Ensure the chair behind your desk is high–backed, swivels**

and has casters. Casters allow for ease of mobility, particularly when you wish to get up quickly. A high–backed chair is also important for those occasions when you need authority, credibility and professionalism. The swivelled, high–back chair also allows you ease of mobility, so that the chair moves when you move. It allows for ease of body movement, particularly upper body movement.

4. **Remove mountains of paperwork or other large obstructions from your desk before meeting with people.** An uncluttered, organized desk allows you to have an unobstructed view of your client. This eliminates any obstruction you have of your visitor's body language. You should position the client chair far enough from the desk to be able to read your visitor's body language and close enough to the desk so that they don't feel alienated from you.
5. **If your office space is large enough and you use it frequently for all manner of discussions, bring in a round table.** The table doesn't have to be large. It can be the type of table that seats two or three people. The benefit of using a round table is that it moves the interaction from role–to–role towards person–to–person. Round tables facilitate an informal meeting or discussion and conversation flows very well. People are more relaxed, and feel more comfortable and at ease. This is a particularly useful strategy when someone comes to see you with a rather personal or confidential issue. It is much easier for them to share a confidence with you when the authoritative barrier of your desk doesn't impede the flow of conversation.
6. **When sitting at the round table, you should sit where you personally can't see your desk.** Barry Triller, the Executive Vice–President of Retail Operations, Sun Life Canada, is a very competent and highly effective executive. For as long as I have known Barry, nearly seven years now, he has always been organ-

ized. His desk is spotless. He disciplines himself to work on one thing at a time and to give that particular task his full attention. When we spoke, we sat at a round table away from his desk. He chose a chair that deliberately blocked his view of his desk. Barry explained that when he is giving an interview, he wants his full focus, concentration and energy directed at that interview. If he looks at his desk, then his concentration and focus are broken by thoughts of incoming e–mails or unfinished work. In order to prevent his concentration from shifting to the mountains of e–mails and other demands of his work, he deliberately keeps his back to his desk. I will never forget the energy and enthusiasm with which he spoke. He certainly wasn't a man distracted by his work during that interview. Barry indicated that he uses the round table extensively in his work as it puts people at ease, facilitates discussions and generally fosters better communication.

7. **Keep a box of Kleenex in your desk at all times.** Unobtrusively handing over a box of Kleenex during an emotional interchange is much better than getting up and leaving the room in search of them right in the middle of the interchange.
8. **Decorate your office in such a manner that it is a reflection of your professional accomplishments.** When you walk into your office, you should feel some sense of pleasure and pride at your accomplishments. Have your degrees, diplomas, certificates and/or awards on the wall. Put up some pictures to give the room some colour and cheer. Bring in a nice plant and some books. Remember that with decorating, less is more. Don't have a gallery of photographs, just two or three to spark initial discussion and conversation. If you don't have a green thumb, I recommend a well–made silk plant in a clay pot covered with some Spanish moss. Plants tend to soften the harsh lines of standard office issue furni-

ture and give the room some character. Once again, less is more. Some people have their offices looking like a greenhouse. This is distracting. Remember, the key impression your office gives to those who enter is that you are a competent, knowledgeable professional who takes pride in their work.

9. **Get a meeting room whenever possible.** Some offices are too small to accommodate more than two people. In order to avoid feeling cramped and uncomfortable, book a meeting room which comfortably seats everyone.
10. **Turn laptop of desk–top computer screens away from your client and away from you.** This minimizes the distractions you will have when speaking to your client. I had a meeting with the President of a company last month. Her laptop computer was on her desk and each time the computer received an e–mail, there was a subtle change in the screen. Her eye kept moving to the screen every few minutes, and I felt as though I was intruding on her time. It was very disconcerting.

PERSONS VS. NON–PERSONS

The need for personal space and the resistance to the invasion of personal space is so strong that, even in a crowd, each member will demand a given amount of space. Herbert Jacobs, a journalist, studied aerial photographs of crowds where he could actually count heads. He concluded that people in dense crowds need six to eight square feet each, while people in loose crowds require an average of ten square feet.

On the subject of crowds, it is important to realize that the personal territory of the people in a crowd is destroyed by the very act of crowding. The reaction to this destruction can, in some cases, change the temper of the crowd. People react very strongly when their personal space or territory is invaded. As a crowd gets larger, tighter and more compact, it tends to also get uglier.

The following true story will illustrate this even further:

> *The news spread like wildfire. A police officer had been killed. In just twenty minutes, the white population was armed and heading for the cabin. Men and mere boys, some not more than 12 years old, carried rifles, shotguns and pistols.*
>
> *The mob, now about four hundred, surrounded the log cabin of a local black man. Tying a rope around the man's neck, they dragged him to the centre of town. While the men argued about the best way to kill him, the women and children shouted their advice — some to hang him, others to burn him alive.*
>
> *Someone pulled a large wooden box out of a store and placed it in the centre of the street. Others filled it with straw. Then they lifted the man, the rope still around his neck, and shoved him head first into the box. One of the men poured oil over him. Another lit a match.*
>
> *As the flames shot upward, the man managed to lift himself out of the box, his body a mass of flames. Trying to shield his face and eyes from the fire, he ran the length of the rope, about twenty feet, when someone yelled, "Shoot!" In an instant, dozens of shots rang out. Men and boys walked to the lifeless body and emptied their guns into it.*
>
> *They dragged the man's body back to the burning box, then piled on more boxes from the stores and poured oil over them. Each time someone threw more oil onto the flames, the crowd roared shouts of approval.*
>
> *Standing about seventy–five feet away, I could smell the poor man's burning flesh. No one tried to hide their*

identity. I could clearly see town officials help in the burning. The inquest, dutifully held by the coroner, concluded that the man met death "at the hands of an enraged mob unknown to the jury." What else could he conclude? Any jury from this town would include men who had participated in the man's death.

They dug a little hole at the edge of the street, and dumped in it the man's ashes and what was left of his body.

The man's name was Sam Pettie, known by everybody to be quiet and inoffensive. I can't mention my name. If I did, I would be committing suicide.

— A May 1914 letter to *The Crisis*

Why did the people in this little town "go mad"? These men — and the women and children who watched in agreement and urged them on — were ordinary, law–abiding citizens. Even some "pillars of the community" joined in the vicious killing of Sam Pettie, who may have been *innocent*.

Psychologists refer to it as "collective behaviour." I'd like to explain this behaviour using proxemics. The personal territory of the people in a crowd is destroyed by the very act of crowding. Once their sense of territory is destroyed, so too is their sense of personal integrity and personal conduct. They stop seeing themselves as one person and become a non–person in a crowd. They no longer have to take responsibility for their own behaviour and actions. They know that their actions aren't judged as their own, but as a member of the crowd. The very fact that they are now crowded makes them feel as though they are a non–person.

The police are also well aware of this fact and they take advantage of it in their interrogation of suspects. A textbook on criminal interrogation and confessions suggests that the questioner sit close to the suspect and that there be no table or other obstacle between them. Any kind of table or other obstacle, the text warns, gives the suspect being questioned a certain degree of relief and confidence because his interpersonal space is not being violated.

The book also suggests that the questioner, though he may start with his chair two or three feet away, should move in closer as the questioning proceeds, so that "ultimately one of the suspect's knees is just about in between the interrogator's two knees."

This physical invasion of the suspect's territory by the police officer, the crowding in as he is questioned, has been found in practice to be extremely useful in breaking down a suspect's resistance. The resounding lesson here is that when a person's interpersonal space is intruded upon, his/her self–assurance tends to grow weaker.

If you are selling to a "buying committee" or to a large group of people, you will need to break through the challenge of not being able to relate to one person at a time but rather, to the group as a whole. Here are some techniques to increase your effectiveness when selling to large groups:

1. Make frequent individual eye contact. Let each person in the room know that you are speaking to them. Let your eyes rest on each person for a few seconds and then move to another person and do the same.
2. Use people's names to make a personal connection.
3. If possible, move around during your presentation to get a non–verbal connection to different members of the audience.
4. Find a reason to hand something to them as it will establish a personal connection. Engage social niceties such as "Please" and "Thank–you."
5. Find a reason to tell a personal anecdote or personal application of your product or service. This helps them see you as an individual.

CHAPTER 5
BEHAVIOUR MODIFICATION EXERCISES

1. Re–arrange your office as directed in this chapter. Find three articles that symbolize your professional achievements and place them where they are visible to both you and your clients.
2. Unclutter your workspace once a quarter.
3. Personalize your office so that it reflects your individuality.
4. Update the pictures of your family members every year or two. Pictures over three years old are dated and are unfair to the ones you love.

CHAPTER 6:

Kinesics — Gestures and Movements

"To listen is to move. To listen is to be moved by the talker — physically and psychologically... The non-moving, unblinking person can reliably be estimated to be a non-listener... When other visible moving has ceased and the eye-blink rate has fallen to less than once in six seconds, listening for practical purposes, has stopped."

— Ernst, Who's Listening?

"I can listen to someone without hearing him. Listening is fixing my attention only on the other person. Hearing requires that I listen inside me as I listen to him. Hearing is a rhythm whereby I shuttle between his words and my experience. It includes hearing his entire posture: his eyes, his lips, the tilt of his head, the movement of his fingers. It includes hearing his tone of voice and his silences. And hearing also includes attending to my reactions, such as the 'sinking feeling' I get when the other person has stopped hearing me."

— Hugh Prather

Kinesics is the term used to refer to bodily movements. It includes such things as facial expression, posture, characteristics of movements and gestures. Kinesics, however, isn't just a fancy communications term. Successful salespeople use kinesics to their advantage routinely. A good salesperson, as I have said before, understands people even more than they understand the intricacies of their product.

The psychology of buying clearly demonstrates that a person's wallet is only opened once their hearts are opened. Whether they are buying life insurance or lingerie, women's clothing or water coolers, cosmetics or computers, people *buy* with their hearts. They only *pay* with their wallets.

This said, exceptional salespeople understand that they are the fundamentally important link between their customer's wallets and their customer's hearts. Body language is the key that unlocks both.

If you think that the words in your sales presentations are so effective, so well–written, so magnetic that they alone are sufficient to sell the product, then why aren't companies screaming these words from the corporate rooftops of North America and throwing the products out the window into the waiting arms of the buying public?

It is Sales Professionals, with all their humanity and their use of body language, their smiles, their gestures, their unique features that sell products. People sell products. Words don't sell products. Successful salespeople allow their humanity to be seen by their clients. It is this unique humanity that we all possess that unlocks the human heart.

Remember at all times that non–verbal communication is 90% of the message. As a Sales Professional, you leverage the verbal message by a factor of nine when you master how to modify your non–verbal communicators.

Never be afraid to use your body to convey your excitement, your passion, your enthusiasm, your dedication and your confidence. *That* is what people are buying. They are buying your excitement about the car. They are buying the admiration in your eyes when they buy your clothes, jewellery or lingerie. They are buying your enthusiasm about the healthy lifestyle they will have once they start taking those vitamins. Let them see your enthusiasm. Let them feel the excitement that emanates from you when you are describing your product. Let them see the vibrancy of your excitement. *That, folks, is kinesics. That, folks, is body language!*

People don't just buy products. They buy dreams, hopes and they buy promises. That is what you sell. What better profession could you have chosen? How better to impact people's lives?

The best salespeople are those who have watched unsuccessful salespeople and have taken the time to understand and appreciate why those people are unsuccessful.

Usually, unsuccessful salespeople are inattentive listeners. Inattentive listeners move their bodies in response to stimuli that are unrelated to the speaker. Their distraction is demonstrated by their body language:

1. Fiddling with pencils or keys
2. Jingling loose change in their pockets
3. Fidgeting nervously
4. Drumming fingers on table–tops
5. Crackling knuckles
6. Frequently shifting weight
7. Crossing and uncrossing the legs
8. Swinging a crossed leg up and down
9. Watching a TV program while being spoken to
10. Waving or nodding one's head to people passing by
11. Continuing with one's activities, like reading the paper

These are all non–verbal behaviours, some of which are reflexive and some of which aren't, which send a message about how well we are listening to our clients and prospects. This type of body language screams not only inattention, but a complete lack of caring for the client. This salesperson is impatient to make the sale and make a quick getaway. He or she will not invest the time to better understand the client and the specific needs of the client. The client, in this instance, is just a means to an end.

I have seen many an unsuccessful salesperson commit exactly those above–outlined sins, as I am sure, have you. It is this type of salesperson that gives all salespeople a bad name. It is this *lack* of attentive listening, this obvious *lack* of sales skill that has created the negative stereotype of the "pushy" or "aggressive" salesperson.

A salesperson who understands the importance of appropriate body movement while listening will, at all costs, *avoid the distracting motions and gestures that ineffective listeners have* and incorporate, instead, the essential skills for effective listening and attending.

HAND GESTURES

In all of my interviews with successful Sales Executives and Sales Professionals, I noticed one thing common to all of them – they spoke using their hands. Their hands would automatically and naturally move when they spoke. Their hands moved when they were making a particularly salient point. They moved when they were excited. They moved when they were happy. They moved without them even realizing that their hands were moving. It was wonderful watching all of these people whose passion and excitement towards their work was so clearly demonstrated by the way they moved.

Many people don't quite know what to do with their hands during social interactions. As a result, their hands are often stuffed into the pockets of their jackets or pants and stay there jingling loose change while they speak. We have all witnessed this.

Using *appropriate* hand gestures not only increases the attention of the listener, it also makes the speaker appear more intelligent and confident. It is important, therefore, to distinguish between *appropriate* hand gestures and *inappropriate* hand gestures.

Inappropriate Hand Gestures: Diminish the impact of your words

1. Fidgeting with pencils or keys or any other objects on the desk while speaking.
2. Drumming your fingers on the table. You are perceived as impatient.
3. Jingling money in your trousers. This unconscious behaviour gives the impression that you have financial worries or troubles.
4. Cracking your knuckles is very disruptive, especially if your knuckles crack very loudly. It gives the listener the impression that you are uncomfortable with what you are saying.
5. Picking at any part of your face. Don't let your hands touch your face when you are speaking to people. This body language, unconscious though it may be, says to your listener, *"Don't pay any attention to what I am saying. Pay attention to what I am doing."* Picking at your face distracts the listener from the impact of your words.
6. Swiping repeatedly and/or scratching your nose. Many studies indicate that the unconscious covering of the mouth in particular and swiping or rubbing at the nose conveys someone "covering up the truth." Research shows that every time someone lies, their blood pressure goes up, causing the blood vessels in their nose to expand. This creates the sensation of itchiness or discomfort in the nose, thus causing us to scratch it or swipe at it. When I see someone swiping at their nose repeatedly while they are speaking to me or to a large audience, I immediately think their bodies are saying, *"Don't pay attention to what I am saying. Pay attention to what I am doing. My actions are distracting you from my words."*
7. Tugging repeatedly at your ears. I had a Sales Professional from a high–end vitamin company speak to me about various health care supplements that would enhance my energy, lengthen my life and add lustre to my appearance. I'll pay anything for that!

Throughout the sales presentation, he pulled at his left ear repeatedly. I really had to concentrate to listen to his presentation and, many times, my eyes and attention were drawn to the repeated pulling of his ear. I didn't buy the supplements. Something about the way he tugged at his ear told me that his body was saying, *"Don't pay attention to what I am saying. Pay attention to what I am doing. My actions are distracting you from my words."*

8. Some women have the annoying tendency of flicking their hair from side to side or running their fingers repeatedly through their hair. Running your fingers through your hair or flicking it from side to side is called *preening behaviour.* Birds and ducks preen themselves by fluffing up their feathers. They do this often during mating season to attract the opposite sex. Interestingly, the same is true of humans. When a woman fluffs up her hair, flicks her hair or does anything that involves running her fingers through her hair, it draws attention to herself, most times, unwittingly. Many women who flick their hair are doing so to remove it from their face. Nonetheless, it is a distracting movement and says to the listener, *"Don't pay attention to what I am saying. Pay attention to how attractive I am. My actions are distracting you from my words."* You can't deny biology. When you move both hands to your head and run your fingers through your hair, the listener's attention will invariably be drawn to your breasts, which are automatically accentuated with this particular hand gesture. It sends a less than professional message.
9. Fidgeting with rings, bracelets and other jewellery is also considered *preening behaviour* and distracts the listener from what you are saying.
10. Pointing at the person. People the world over find it offensive when someone points to them and speaks. It sends the message that the speaker doesn't respect the listener and can also lead to conflict because many people feel "put down" when pointed at.

As you can see, inappropriate hand gestures *detract* from the power of your presentations. Unfortunately, many of these hand gestures are unconscious movements. Great care must be taken to ensure that your body movements are effective and enhance the power of your words.

Appropriate Hand Gestures: Increase the Impact of Your Words

1. Use your hands to steeple your fingers (see Illustration #1) when speaking. This solves the problem of what to do with your hands. The **steepling** gesture is very powerful. It says, *"I can be trusted," "I have personal integrity," "I believe strongly in what I am saying and stand behind my product."* It is easy to remember why the act of steepling works so effectively. When you steeple your fingers, they look like the steeple of a church, and this enables you to borrow prestige and authority, the same way church buildings do. Steepling is particularly useful when you are dealing with clients who are resistant to being sold. Sales Professionals are often advisors and consultants on a range of issues, be it fashion, image, finance, or health. In order to have your customers interact with you in a manner that suggests that you are imparting useful advice, steeple your hands. The steepling gesture is particularly effective when you are sitting at a desk (see Illustration #2).
2. Use your hands to emphasize your points (see Illustration #3). When you are standing, keep your hands around the middle of your body, between your stomach and hips. When sitting, especially at your desk, remember that your upper body is what the client sees. As such, it is important that your hands be used when you speak.
3. Keep your fingers spread open a bit, as opposed to having them close against each other. This gives the impression that you are confident and lends an air of authenticity to your movements.

Your hand gestures look more genuine if your fingers aren't pressed too tightly together.

4. Keep your fingernails trimmed or manicured so that the length of the nail isn't too long or too short. For men, keep a white–band width of approximately 1.5 mm. For women, if you do have long nails, colour the nail flesh tone and keep the vibrant colours for evening wear. Long nails with vibrant colours can distract your listeners, especially if adorned with sparkles, rainbows, diamond studs, *etc.* (I'm not joking, I've seen it all!).

Your hands are a great expression of who you are. The important thing to remember when using your hands is to be genuine. If you aren't someone who traditionally uses your hands when you speak, then, by all means, take small steps. Start by removing your hands from your pockets and keep them comfortably at your side. Practise using your hands when speaking in front of a mirror. When you next use the phone to speak to anyone, speak in front of a mirror and *use your hands* for emphasis. You will notice that your voice will immediately become more powerful and have greater expression.

The change should be gradual but progressive. Practise gesturing with your hands until it becomes habit to do so.

HANDSHAKES

Make it a point to shake people's hands routinely. A good solid grip and two up and down shakes are generally the way North Americans shake hands and expect their hands to be shaken. Shaking hands is another gesture that varies from culture to culture and may have strong cultural/historical significance. South Americans tend to shake hands more vigorously, frequently, and for a longer period of time.

Interestingly, most cultures use the right hand when shaking. Since most of the population of the world is right–handed, this may

Illustration #1

Illustration #2

Illustration #3

not be surprising. However, some researchers believe that shaking with the right hand may be a symbolic act of peace, as in older times it was the right hand that generally held the weapons.

In some Muslim and Asian countries, touching anyone with the left hand may be considered an obscenity (the left hand is an aid to the process of elimination or "unclean," while the right one is used for the intake of food or "clean"). Offering something with the left hand to a Muslim may be an insult of the most serious type.

In the cross–cultural environment in which we work and live, it is important to find a way to connect with people to convey a myriad of messages, especially when neither party can find the words with which to do so. Reaching out to shake someone's hand, particularly someone from another culture, is a wonderful way to bridge the cultural and language gap.

Handshakes convey friendship, positive regard and trust. Although some cultures prefer more vigorous shakes, or shake for a longer period of time, the gesture, in and of itself, means the same throughout virtually all cultures.

Most business interactions commence with a handshake. During the course of my interviews, many Sales Professionals and Sales Executives said that a common problem today is that many females still have a *limp* handshake. Women, especially those of us over 35, have been socialized to shake hands gently so as not to appear too masculine. A limp handshake, however, gives the receiver the sense that you are lacking in confidence and authority. Furthermore, it gives them the impression that they can take advantage of you, because you are perceived as being a "push–over." In order to be perceived as authoritative, confident and command the respect of those with whom you do business, make your handshake firm.

There is a significant difference between a firm grip and a *vice–like* grip. People get angry when their hands are squeezed too hard and held too long, especially North American born clients. Keep the handshake short and don't squeeze too hard. Be mindful that your clients may be wearing rings, and too hard a handshake may cause their rings to dig into their flesh, causing them a fair amount of pain.

SMILING

Emotions are contagious. We feel happy around people who are happy, find ourselves drawn to be near then and to look at them. People who smile routinely are considered to be more attractive, they tend to have more friends, they tend to be promoted faster, and generally consider themselves to be happy, optimistic people.

Our brains are very complex. Every thought we think, every emotion we feel, every sensation we experience, every decision we reach, every move we make — in short, all human behaviour — is rooted in a biological event. All our thoughts, feelings, and behaviour can ultimately be traced to the activity of specialized cells called neurons.

Most experts estimate that there are as many as 100 billion neurons in the brain. This means that you have about 17 times as many neurons as there are people living on this planet right now.

Neurons perform several important tasks: (1) they relay messages from your eyes, ears, nose, mouth and skin to the brain and spinal cord and (2) they act as messengers from the brain and the spinal cord to your muscles and glands so that you can move. "What has this got to do with smiling?" you ask. It's quite simple. When you smile, your neurons send a message to your brain that you are happy. Your brain, having received this message, absorbs this information, and proceeds to let your body (muscles and glands) know that you are happy. When this happens, you are inexplicably happy.

Smiling, even when your general mood is low, will result in an elevation in your mood. Smiling tricks your brain and you can usually proceed from feeling blue to feeling cheerful. Hollywood producers have always known this. Sitcoms and other humorous movies elevate our moods because they make us smile and laugh.

Good Sales Professionals smile habitually. They make it a habit to smile whenever they come into contact with anyone. Two things happen when you smile. First, you radiate confidence and happiness. Everyone wants some of that. Second, you now have *Attraction Power.*

Have you ever noticed how some Sales Professionals have an 80 to 90% closing ratio, while others barely make the 20–30% range. The reason for this is *Attraction Power.* Successful salespeople understand the psychology of attraction at its fundamental level. People are attracted *more* to people who smile. People who smile have magnetism. They attract people with their smile. Their smile radiates their confidence and says, *"I am happy to be helping you and I am enjoying this."* Show your clients that you are having fun and enjoying the experience of serving them. These customers will then become loyal customers and refer people to you based on the good time you showed them.

FEET AND LEG MOVEMENTS

Lower body movements are just as important as those of the upper body. In fact, there are messages that our lower body sends about our interest in what we are doing and our commitment to our work that can't be mimicked by the upper body.

Here are some of those messages.

1. ***In what direction are your feet pointing?*** If your feet are pointing towards the door, then that's where you want to go. If your customer's feet are pointing toward the door, that's where she *will* go. Successful Sales Professionals keep their customers' feet pointing *away* from the door and this increases their psychological commitment to buy. This summer, I was at a furniture store and I noticed that as soon as I stepped inside, a Sales Professional approached me and welcomed me into the store. He

invited me to browse through the store and asked me what, in particular, I was searching for. He encouraged me to walk through the store. I was hooked. Many retail salespeople ask me what they should say to people to encourage them to buy. My answer is, say "Welcome to _________. I am pleased to have you in our fine store. Would you like me to show you around, or would you like to browse on your own?" Make your clients come right into the store. Keep their feet pointing inside, not towards the door.

2. ***Break the "accordion knees" habit.*** Moving your knees in and out like an accordion is not only distracting. In many cases, it is considered vulgar. This is usually an unconscious movement, and many people are shocked when it is brought to their attention that they have "accordion knees." When I see someone, man or woman, doing this, three things come to mind. The first is that this person is childish. The second is that this person has poor impulse control. The third and most salient thought that goes through people's minds is that this person is impatient. When your clients have accordion knees it is a signal for you to wrap up quickly as they are getting tired of waiting and are anxious to be off.
3. ***Crossing and uncrossing of the legs.*** Women more than men experience this particular challenge. This, too, is an unconscious, almost reflexive action. Constant crossing and uncrossing of your legs is very distracting for the listener, especially when you are wearing an outfit that shows your legs. Once again, it sends the message that you would like your listener to *"Pay more attention to what I am doing than what I am saying."* It also conveys a restlessness that suggests that you are uncomfortable in your own skin.
4. ***Swinging a crossed leg up and down.*** This is also an unconscious, almost reflexive action that many women do. It is very

distracting and has the added danger that it sends more of a sensual message than a professional one. The message conveyed by this action is that you want your listener to *pay greater attention to your legs than to what you are saying.* I don't recommend crossing your legs when you are seated. I feel that it is more professional to sit with your knees close together and your feet close together. It is a neat, stream–lined look, and gives the added impression that you are a neat, organized, efficient person. Leg swinging is also considered *"preening behaviour."* While this action works wonders at a bar, it diminishes your professionalism.

The language spoken by your body is much louder and more powerful than the words spoken from your mouth. Our mouths lie effortlessly. Our bodies, however, routinely speak the truth.

Let your gestures reflect your honesty, integrity and confidence. Take care to control and manage your body's gestures, both voluntary and reflexive. You control the image that your body portrays. Pay close attention to what your gestures are telling people about *who you are and what you are.*

CHAPTER 6
BEHAVIOUR MODIFICATION EXERCISES

Now we are at the stage of putting it all together. The following exercises are demanding, but very useful and have tremendous impact on your presentations.

1. Videotape your sales interview with a colleague or your sales manager. Watch it with them and identify one non-verbal habit that *reduces* your effectiveness. Then identify the two things you are doing best.
2. Repeat the above exercise. This time, look for one other non-verbal habit that you wish to change, and *two* that you wish to *reinforce.*
3. Have a conversation with your significant other in the TV room, but with the television turned off. Speak together for at least 20 minutes. The purpose of this exercise is to read each other's gestures and movements to enhance your non-verbal communication towards each other.
4. On your next five prospecting phone calls, use exaggerated hand movements to heighten your effectiveness.
5. The easiest and most powerful principle you can take from this handbook is the importance of smiling. For the next three hours deliberately smile more than you normally would and watch the reaction of people around you.

CHAPTER 7:

Haptics — To Touch or Not to Touch?

Making or failing to make body contact is another form of nonverbal communication. Such communication through touching behaviour is called *haptics.*

Perhaps no other area of nonverbal communication is fraught with more ambivalence and conflicting opinions than touching or being touched by another. Our need for touch — what Ashley Montagu (1971) has termed "skin hunger" — is abiding. Yet *how* we go about gratifying our "hunger" for touch has emerged as a very controversial area.

According to Julia Wood (1993), behaviour, including touching, that was once regarded as flirtatious, natural, and complimentary has undergone considerable scrutiny. The same behaviour, in certain instances, is often now viewed as "unwanted, unwelcome, unprofessional, and unacceptable." It is important to understand one undisputable fact: there is an immense power behind physical contact. Human beings need physical contact. The key, then, is to develop the right or appropriate touch in our daily lives.

Do you get uncomfortable if a stranger touches you? Many of us do. Just as we observe unwritten rules about speaking distance, so too, we learn rules about touching from our culture.

Not only does *frequency* of touching differ across cultures, but so does the *meaning* of touching within a culture. In general, higher-status individuals do more touching. You are much more likely to see teachers touch students and bosses touch administrative assistants than the other way around. In many countries and in many cultures, it is considered unseemly or inappropriate for lower-status individuals to put their hands on their superiors.

Most outstanding salespeople have mastered the art of establishing rapport though non-sensual touch.

An interesting experiment with surgery patients illustrates how touching can have different meanings. When the nurse came in to tell patients about their upcoming surgery and aftercare, she touched the patients twice, once briefly on the arm when she introduced herself, and then for a full minute on the arm during the instruction period. When she left, she shook each patient's hand.

Men and women reacted very differently to this. Touching *lowered the blood pressure and anxiety* of the women, both before the surgery and for more than an hour afterward. The touching upset the men, however. Their *blood pressure and anxiety rose.* One way of interpreting these findings is that, perhaps, North American men find it harder to acknowledge dependency and fear than women do. For men, then, instead of a comfort, a well-intentioned touch may be a threatening reminder of their vulnerability.

Another way of looking at these findings is to acknowledge that a relationship exists between haptics and dominance. Those people with higher power are more likely to touch their subordinates than they are to be touched by their subordinates. Consequently, when a person touches another, it may not be a message of increasing intimacy but, instead, of dominance.

There is a strong perception that women receive more touch and are touched more by men because they are generally regarded as weaker and more vulnerable. In the surgery example, one explanation for the elevated blood pressure and anxiety by the male patients may be due to the fact that the nurse was female, and she *initiated* the touch. The touch was *prolonged* and *uninvited.* These men may have felt discomfort due to the sudden change of status.

Touch has many meanings: warmth, affection, interest, or encouragement versus anger, dominance, or abuse. Whether touch is reciprocal (initiated by both parties) or unilateral (initiated by one party), depends on several factors:

1. The relationship of the parties involved (*e.g.* parent and child, husband and wife, employer and employee, doctor and patient)
2. The age of the individuals
3. The context of the interaction (*e.g.* the home, the workplace, a social or sporting event)
4. The cultural attitude toward touching behaviour

The act of touching another individual is open to diverse interpretation and can serve to *defuse* conflict or to *create* conflict. Although touch is often interpreted as an attempt to affiliate, to encourage, or to empathize with another person — acts that are very constructive in managing and defusing conflict — it can also reflect efforts to *control* or to *impose* one's will on another.

<u>Taboo Touches in the Workplace</u>

1. Unwanted sexual touches
2. Touches overly friendly for the relationship or situation
3. Inappropriate power plays
4. Touches that disrupt or interfere with work tasks

Such touching behaviour may create a hostile work environment and lead to allegations of harassment.

To avoid these potential allegations, many companies have attempted to formulate policies that would prohibit touch in the workplace. Stanley Jones, the author of *The Right Touch: Understanding and Using the Language of Physical Contact* (1995) explains why these efforts may be misdirected:

Despite such concerns and attitudes, seeing touch in the workplace as a problem to be eliminated is not realistic. The impulse to touch simply does not go away when people put on a suit. In fact, in some ways the workplace environment creates special needs for touch... [T]here are numerous legitimate reasons for touching in the office. The awareness of being evaluated on an ongoing basis means that touches of support and encouragement are especially wanted. Touch is also a legitimate and effective way of persuading others, and exerting influence is an integral part of work. In addition, many people see their work activity as an opportunity for social contacts that may carry over outside the office, and friendly exchanges can also enhance working relationships; both of these motivations encourage touching.

The question is not whether people will or should touch in the office. They will and they should. The question is, what are the real barriers to touch, the ones that should not be crossed?

I would argue that in order to determine "the real barriers to touch," it is important for men and women to examine carefully both their motivations for touching and their responses when others touch them.

<u>Appropriate motivations for touching in the workplace:</u>

1. Lending support and encouragement to a co-worker or client who is in need

2. Reassure and console someone during times of crisis
3. Building trust and confidence in someone

Men and women have varying degrees of comfort with touching and being touched. Women, in general, are more comfortable hugging other women. I have spoken at many conferences where the population base was mainly women, especially in the Direct Sales industry — companies like Weekender's Clothing, Partylite Gifts, Mary Kay Cosmetics, and Avon, all of which employ Direct Sales Professionals, the majority of whom are women.

At the Weekender's Conference, for example, I noticed that these women greeted each other with a hug. These hugs, rather than being perceived as sexually motivated, are a means of lending support and encouragement, solidifying friendships and expressing their enthusiasm for seeing each other. I noticed the same at the Partylite Gifts Conference as well. These women, all of whom are very successful Sales Professionals, use touch to encourage, empathize, build trust, show support, and propel each other to greater successes.

It is quite common for men to hug and kiss each other in Arab countries as a method of displaying respect and admiration. Increasingly, we are seeing men hugging when receiving public praise or acknowledgement. Likely, this is a carry-over from the sports world where teams of men routinely hug to celebrate a teammates success. Witness the hugging that occurs between team members as soon as a goal is scored at a hockey game.

I interviewed Bob Barr, a Regional Vice-President for Clarica, a subsidiary of Sun Life Financial. Bob has hired and trained many women. Quite a number of his direct reports are women. I brought up the subject of touching in the workplace, and asked him what his thoughts were. His responses were very helpful. Bob's region is located in Western Canada. Many of his direct reports fly from Vancouver, Victoria and Alberta to his office in Waterloo. He also flies out to their locations. When they greet him, many of the female members of his team hug him. Bob acknowledged that, at first, he had to get used to this, as he initially wasn't accustomed to hugging people in the office.

He indicated that he respects these women a great deal for their hard work, commitment and intelligence. He complimented them repeatedly on their personal integrity and determination to achieve their team goals. He was keenly aware of the tremendous sense of teamwork they all shared. It was obvious to me that Bob enjoyed working with these women and held them in very high regard.

His one salient piece of advice to women and men is to be aware that "people need their space, and if you do hug, keep it quick." He explained that he prefers using a "firm hand-shake" but if people prefer to hug, his advice is to "keep it quick."

Many male Business Executives prefer not to hug their female co-workers. Their preference is a firm, quick handshake. This way, at no time is their sense of space being violated. This said, in the event that a male and female do hug in the workplace, the most effective, business-like way of hugging is the A-frame hug.

The A-frame Hug

In the A-frame hug, both parties stand with their feet at the bottom components of the A, and their upper bodies meet at the apex, just like an A. The hug is brief, with contact at the shoulders. It serves to lend support, encourage, be sympathetic, congratulate, greet people and is also suitable for leave-taking. The A-frame hug is the best workplace hug between men and women. Because the lower and mid-regions of your bodies never touch, it can not be misconstrued as sexual. The key is to "keep it quick."

When meeting someone for the first time, especially a client from a different culture, there are two things to keep in mind:

1. If it is a couple from a different culture, shake hands with the male and read the body language of the female *before* you reach out to shake hands. A friend of mine had an interesting experience when she met a Chinese couple in order to sell them some financial products. Both my friend and her manager are also Chinese. She and her manager went to the couple's home to discuss their family's insurance needs. Her Manager shook the gentleman's hand, and when he attempted to shake the woman's hand, *she stepped back.* Gauge the response of the female client prior to shaking her hand. If she is smiling and welcoming you into her home, take note of whether she steps forward to meet you. If she steps forward and she acts welcoming, chances are she will be receptive to a handshake. If, however, she remains rooted behind her husband and doesn't move forward, then smile and thank her for the courtesy of her time, but do not attempt to shake her hand.
2. Always use your right hand to shake hands, even if you are left-handed. If the client initiates the handshake, and he or she is left-handed, and they use their left hand to initiate, then follow suit. Keep in mind that people from any of the Muslim countries will always shake hands using their right hand. Be prepared in either eventuality.
3. There are some cultures that tend to shake hands more vigorously, frequently and for a longer period of time. An example of this is the Spanish culture. Removing your hand too quickly in this instance will give the impression that you are aloof, cold and unfriendly. Be mindful of these cultural differences and try to adapt to their communication style by lengthening your handshake, giving it more vigour and shaking hands more frequently when dealing with those cultures.

If you were going to a foreign country for a vacation and you planned on spending a couple of weeks in this country, chances are you would take the time to buy a dictionary of terms and phrases, just to increase your communication skills in that foreign language. You would learn phrases like, "Where is the washroom?" and "Do you take Visa or American Express?" or "Thank you" and "You're welcome." Learning to speak these simple phrases in the native language of the country you are visiting would make communication much easier and faster, wouldn't it?

Of course it would. Learning the basics of a language enhance your enjoyment of the whole experience because you know that you have been understood.

This is the essence of communication. Enhanced understanding of our fellow human being only comes when we seek to learn the language of others, as well as our own.

Really effective Sales Professionals learn to use touch unobtrusively. They understand the importance of building an emotional connection with their clients, and the impact this emotional connection makes to solidify the sale.

CHAPTER 7
BEHAVIOUR MODIFICATION EXERCISES

1. Practise shaking hands with your manager and several of your colleagues. Use a firm grip, but do not squeeze. Press your thumb firmly against the person's skin during the handshake. Do they notice the impact of your handshake?
2. When you are shaking hands, use your other hand to gently touch the person on their elbow. You will need to curve your left elbow and also change your body posture to do this effectively. If you are shaking with your right hand, touch the person's right elbow using your left hand. Do this lightly and unobtrusively. Do you notice the instant connection you make? Practise doing this until it is seamless and genuine.
3. Many of your clients will have pets. Provided that you aren't allergic to them, giving a pet a friendly pat on the head or scratching them behind the ears, as long as you are gentle, will not only endear the pet to you, it will also endear the client to you.
4. People also like it when you notice their children and call them by name. Shake the hands of the children you meet, and use their name in the conversational interchange.

CHAPTER 8:

Presenting with Power, Authority and Confidence

When asked to rate, in order of importance, their ten greatest fears in life, people listed death as #3! Guess where they listed Public Speaking? That's right, at #1. People would rather die than speak in public.

The majority of people detest public speaking. Their blood pressure rises, their heart races, they experience tremendous gastrointestinal discomfort, their knees shake, their voices tremble, and generally, they can't wait to get it over with as quickly as possible.

We have all had our fair share of Public Presenters who stand up in front of the lectern, keep their eyes firmly on their speech, read their speech as quickly and unenthusiastically as possible and rush off the stage to the safety of their chair. Those speeches are unbearable to sit through and do nothing to hold our attention. We would be hard-pressed to remember the general message of their speech and even harder-pressed to remember what the speaker looked like. Unfortunately, this is a common problem.

When asked to give a speech, many people spend most or all of their time preparing the *words* of their speech. They write it and re-write it. They *read* it to themselves. They practice *reading* it in front of their colleagues. They *read* it to their spouses, their children, and even their pets. Finally, on the night of the speech, they *read* it to their audiences. It is an excruciating experience, both for the speaker *and* for the audience.

In order for a speech to have high impact and entertain audiences to the point where they are laughing and clapping and really enjoying the presentations the speaker has to do *much* more than read his script. The speaker has to *perform!*

Public speaking has much more to do with performing and acting than it actually has to do with speaking. And it has little or nothing to do with reading. The important thing to remember when speaking in front of people is that people generally have the attention span of a MuchMusic video. They will listen to you if you are interesting to look at, have something interesting to say and present in a dynamic and exciting manner. They won't listen to you if you look drab, your topic holds no interest for them, and your delivery is monotonous.

Captivating people when you speak to them is as much an art as it is a science. There are several important competencies that you must master before you can fascinate and delight your audiences. These competencies can be broken down into four categories:

1. Technical preparation
2. Physical preparation
3. Emotional and Mental preparation
4. Delivery

All four of these categories, in conjunction, work to effectively command the attention of your audience. It is impossible to ignore categories one, two, and three and expect your delivery to be perfect.

Each category must be followed in the order in which it is presented.

STEP 1: TECHNICAL PREPARATION

Winston Churchill once said, "If you want me to speak for 5 hours, give me 5 minutes preparation; if you want me to speak for 5 minutes, give me 5 weeks to prepare."

Most people have to speak within an allotted time frame. Very rarely does someone have to speak for more than one hour. However, no matter what your time allotment, respect your audience by not exceeding it. People find it very difficult sitting still for long periods of time, and you will lose their attention if you speak for longer than they are expecting you to.

Own your script. It is not enough to read what you have written to the audience. In point of fact, your audience will know if you are unfamiliar with your script. Your pauses will be filled with a number of "ums" and "ahs" and you won't be comfortable using planned silences. Your paralanguage, especially your tone, will not be effective if you read. When people read, they tend to look down at their sheets of paper. Their voice, therefore, doesn't project towards the audience. Instead, it flows down, towards the paper. Memorize your script. Learn it to such an extent that you can say it in your sleep. Once you have memorized your script, "professionalize" your script. This is where you put in the pauses, the planned silences and the special touches that make it sound as though you are saying it to the audience for the very first time. The audience doesn't hear your recitation as a memorized speech. It sounds more like you are speaking to them.

"Professionalizing" your script is the difference between watching a professional performance of King Lear, as seen at the Stratford Festival or on Broadway, and seeing the Grade 7 rendition of it. Both sets of performers know their lines, both sets of performers speak their lines. The difference is in how they portray the characters.

The professional performers at the Stratford Festival and on Broadway not only "professionalize" their scripts, they "personalize" them as well. Every word sounds as if it's being said for the first time. There is a sense of "newness" to the words. Voices resonate across the stage. You can hear the passion, emotion and energy that radiates with every spoken word.

Owning your script means that you take it from mere memorization, professionalize it and finally, personalize it.

If you are using a PowerPoint presentation, here are a few very important things to remember:

1. Less is more. Put no more than 30 words on each page.
2. Have some slides that have only one word or image on it.
3. Make your point verbally and *then* put on the slide in case someone in the audience had difficulty following your original point or was sleeping through it.
4. Concise wording on slides is much better than long sentences — no one reads the long sentences.
5. Use illustrations or comic cartoons to make your point — humour is very powerful.
6. People love pictures — they are visual and are much more interesting to look at than words.
7. Use graphs sparingly. They are usually too technical and complicated for people to follow.
8. While you are speaking, keep the screen blank.
9. Stand to the left-hand side of the screen (from the perspective of your audience). People read from left to right. Once they have finished reading the screen, their eyes will revert automatically back to you, but if you stand to the right of the screen (from the perspective of the audience) they will finish reading the screen and wonder why they feel restless.
10. Do not use too many slides. Remove extraneous slides from your

final product. Remember that people's eyes get very fatigued if they have to keep looking at slides.

11. Remove the special effects with the little stick man doing a dance, or the waving flags. It detracts from the message and is very visually distracting.
12. Use large fonts so that people in the back of the room can read the words.

Do a run-through of your presentation in the room where you are expected to speak. Make sure your microphone is at the correct level. Get used to the way sound moves in the room. Sound runs are very important because you can iron out any technical difficulties before you get on stage. Know whether your microphone will be on before you get on stage, or whether you will have to turn it on. If so, learn how to do this before you do your speech.

Ensure that your PowerPoint presentation is set to go when you are. I have watched many presenters struggle with their computers during their speech because they are experiencing "technical difficulties." Have everything at a state of readiness so that all you have to do is to press the button on your remote mouse and your first slide goes on the screen. The most important detail here is to make sure that your remote mouse operates well and has fresh batteries in it. Do a "dry" run with the PowerPoint presentation at least twice to ensure that your slides are all in order.

Unless it is absolutely necessary, don't use a lectern when you speak. Lecterns obstruct the audience's ability to see your body. Lecterns also encourage speakers to look down at their notes instead of at their audience. Have the lectern removed, if possible, for your presentation. It gives the audience a sense that something special is about to happen and they are going to be *presented to* as opposed to *talked at.*

STEP 2: PHYSICAL PREPARATION

How you look is just as important as what you say. You want your appearance to look sharp, commanding and authoritative. There is a uniform worn for public presentations, just as in any other role in life. Here are some suggestions to ensure that your appearance impresses your audience as much as your message does.

1. Dress to complement the audience. Your outfit should be well-pressed and recently dry cleaned. If you are wearing trousers, it is better if they have a sharp crease.
2. Your shirt or blouse should be clean and also very well pressed. Ensure that there are no stains on it, as this will make you self-conscious and detract from your performance.
3. Dress one notch up from your audience. The best way to do that is to wear a dark blazer or suit jacket, preferably one that is the exact colour of your trousers, or skirt, or one that complements your trousers or skirt.
4. Gentlemen, wear a deep red tie. If you aren't fond of deep red, find another colour that is both arresting and highly-authoritative — royal purple for example. Avoid wearing a black tie with a black suit. You will either look like one of the Blues Brothers or an undertaker and it is visually very boring.
5. Ladies, stick with primary colours. Avoid pastel pinks, yellows and greens. They detract from your authority and don't give you the necessary contrast from the stage. Dark blue or black skirt or pant suits with a crisp white or red shirt are good choices.
6. Remove excessive jewellery and/or visible body piercings. Too much jewellery detracts from your authority, and the flashes and twinkles can distract the audience.
7. Ensure that your hair does not fall on your face. Get your hair styled or cut in such a manner that it does not move onto your face so that you have to flick it back into place from time to time.

This gesture is very distracting and it sends the message that you want the audience to *pay more attention to what you are doing and less attention to what you are saying.* Do not touch your hair throughout any of your presentation.

8. Polish your shoes and remove any scuffs. Ladies, ensure that your heels are sturdy enough to support you and that your posture is not affected by heels that are too high or too thin.

STEP 3: EMOTIONAL AND MENTAL PRESENTATION

Just prior to speaking, it is important to centre yourself emotionally and mentally and clear your mind of everything else. You need to take some time to be by yourself. Find a quiet room or corner and spend five or ten minutes entirely by yourself. Visualize yourself speaking powerfully. Visualize your success. Say a few words of encouragement to yourself. Check your appearance in a mirror. Ensure that you are comfortable. Make a trip to the bathroom.

I've watched some excellent speakers in my time. Barry Triller, whom I have quoted many times in this book, has a ritual just before he speaks. He finds a mirror, snaps his fingers and says, "Knock 'em dead, kid!" During his quiet time, Barry focuses on the palms of his hands.

Have a ritual that you perform just before you speak. Follow your ritual every time you are about to speak. Talk to yourself. Encourage yourself. Visualize your success. Go straight from your quiet, centred space to the stage. Do not stop and talk to people on the way up. Smile while you are being introduced and *Go!*

STEP 4: DELIVERY

Walk to the stage with confidence, and a briskness in your step. Many people use theme music or music with a good strong beat as accompaniment when they walk to the stage. This is very powerful and usually gets the audience excited about what is about to happen.

Music changes the energy in the room immediately. This is particularly effective if people have been sitting for long periods of time and are becoming restless.

Every good presenter has his or her own tried and true methods of delivering powerful speeches. One such presenter, Bob Barr, also quoted in Chapter 7, uses these strategies in his delivery:

1. Look out at your audience just before you speak and throughout your speech.
2. Relax and watch their reactions to your words.
3. Play to the audience.
4. Speak to your audience as if you are having a one-sided conversation with them.
5. Use the names of people in the audience in recounting humorous incidents or to give praise.
6. Stay in the moment. Put all your concentration into what you are doing at that time.
7. Instead of taking your entire speech up to the stage, write some key words on a business card and use that to jog your memory should you need it.
8. Smile at your audience. This gives people the sense that you are confident and relaxed as opposed to nervous and uptight.
9. Don't tell jokes to a multicultural audience. Jokes tend to be culturally specific. Some jokes will fall flat because some cultures don't see the humour in it. This doesn't preclude you from being humorous. Certainly, you can make people laugh by taking some licence with someone *who you know will take it well.* Self-deprecating humour is often the best type of humour. This type of humour makes people in the group feel as one.
10. Your timing has to be impeccable. The only way you can ensure that your timing always stays on course is by gauging the mood of your audience and watching their reactions at all times.

11. Maintain eye contact with individual members of your audience throughout your presentation. Let your eyes rest on each member (whenever possible) for a few seconds so that your connection with them will increase.
12. Do not walk from side to side throughout the presentation. It is very distracting. Move slowly if you are going to move on stage, so that people aren't too distracted by your movements.
13. Keep your hands out of your pockets and use them to gesture and emphasize your points.
14. Exaggerate your stage movements and gestures when speaking to a crowd of over 100 people. The people at the back of the room will feel the full effect of your presentation only if you exaggerate your hand gestures and other movements.
15. Engage your audience using your tone. Make sure your voice projects to all corners of the room.
16. Keep your words clear, specific and succinct. Never say "Blah, blah, blah" when "Blah" will do.
17. Make it look like you are having fun. Only when you are relaxed and enjoying yourself will your audience join you by doing the same.
18. Use planned silences. They are very dramatic and lend authority to your statements.

The key to being a powerful presenter is understanding that public speaking is a skill. It is learned and developed only through careful preparation and practice. Very few people are naturally gifted at speaking in public. Everyone has to work at it. Understanding and applying these four categories of technical preparation, physical preparation, emotional/mental preparation and delivery are crucial to successful presentations.

The best speakers are the ones who have practised these skills over a long period of time and are at ease with their audience, themselves and their topics. You too can speak with power, authority and confidence. The key is to practice.

CHAPTER 8
BEHAVIOUR MODIFICATION EXERCISES

1. On paper, outline a presentation in point form. Choose any topic that is of interest to you. Write it out in full and start to memorize it, professionalize it and then personalize it.
2. Write out two humorous anecdotes that happened to you. Practise recounting these anecdotes to yourself and then to a group of people.
3. Visualize yourself making a presentation to a large group of people. How do you look? What are you doing well? What do you feel you need to work on?

CHAPTER 9:

Telephone Success Using Body Language

"Our doubts are traitors,
and make us lose the good we oft might win
by fearing to attempt."
— Shakespeare

Initially, Sales Professionals cringe when their managers tell them that they have to make outbound telephone calls on a daily basis in order to ensure a steady stream of business. They are reluctant to pick up the phone and speak to someone they have never met before to set up an appointment.

Using the phone to increase your activity level is essential for Sales Professionals. The only way you can ensure constant sales activity is by speaking to and seeing a large number of people. The telephone is an excellent vehicle to connect with people.

Successful Sales Professionals are comfortable using the phone on a daily basis. They habitually make outbound prospecting calls to book appointments, and they successfully develop the "call courage" necessary to overcome any resistance they initially encountered.

The great Sales Trainers, Jack and Garry Kinder of Dallas, Texas say that Sales Professionals learn to cope with call reluctance and build call courage by following these suggestions:

1. Stay sold on what you are selling.
2. Saturate your mind with positive thoughts.
3. Prepare yourself technically.
4. Focus on the rewards of success, not on the penalties of failure.
5. Remind yourself that most people are nice people.
6. Let prospects key off of your attitude – never key off of theirs.

Having a positive attitude about who you are, the products you sell, and people in general ensures that your tone of voice is optimistic and upbeat. Let your prospects hear the smile in your voice. Let them hear the confidence with which you describe the technical merits of your product.

Take the Kinder Pledge — *"I will never begin talking to a prospect on the telephone, in a seminar, or on an interview until I have written out my script, rehearsed and learned the lines so that they can be expressed* ***naturally*****,** ***conversationally*** *and* ***persuasively****."*

The best salespeople are the one's who have developed a telephone script that sounds as though they are speaking, not reading. Memorize your script so that it is conversational in nature and use your tone of voice to make it persuasive. Take the time to professionalize and personalize your script.

Stand when you are speaking to people on the phone. Use a cordless phone and walk slowly around the room as you are speaking to people. Standing, as opposed to hunching over your desk, expands your vocal cords. Walking gives your voice higher energy than you have while you are sitting and speaking.

Speak from your diaphragm, not just the back of your throat. As Dwight Powell said in the chapter on Paralanguage, "Make sure your voice has a bottom to it." Make a conscious effort to lower your voice, as that lends it more authority.

Remember, most people are nice people. Most people will speak to you respectfully as long as they are spoken to in that same manner. However, even nice people, when they are interrupted at dinner or from a deep sleep, will be grouchy. Apologize for the bad timing and swiftly get off the phone.

Make a humorous comment when speaking to someone on the phone. You may be the only person who has made them laugh today. Laughter is infectious and it improves people's general disposition and mood. Let them hear the laughter and smile in your voice.

Develop the habit of phoning people daily. Do your phoning at the same time every day if you can. Making outbound telephone calls is not only a necessary component of your profession, telephoning is essential to the ongoing success of your business. Make telephoning a habit. You brush your teeth every day and it is now your habit to do so. The same must be the case for making outbound telephone calls.

As the late Dr. Maxwell Maltz always said, "The surest way to develop courage is to act courageous." Make it a habit to call at least ten prospects daily. By the end of the first call, you will be nervous and your palms may be sweaty. By the end of the tenth call, you will feel much more relaxed. By the end of the first week, you'll wonder why you were nervous in the first place.

CHAPTER 9
BEHAVIOUR MODIFICATION EXERCISES

1. Write out your telephone script, the purpose of which is to get an appointment with your prospect. Professionalize it and personalize it. Make it sound natural and conversational.
2. Practise saying your script out loud. Have you used unfilled pauses and planned silences?
3. Make ten outbound calls every day for five days consecutively. Use your prepared, rehearsed telephone script.

CHAPTER 10:

Conclusion

"A human being always acts and feels and performs in accordance with what he imagines to be true about himself and his environment. This is a basic and fundamental law of the mind. It is the way we are built."

— Dr. Maxwell Maltz

Excellence in sales performance begins with having a strong image of who you are and what you do. Your attitude determines your success. Understand that the biggest sale you will make in your career is the sale to *yourself.* Each and every day in your career you will come across people who will question the usefulness of your product. Unless you "stay sold on what you are saying" you will not be able to deal with their objections.

You may have the loftiest of goals, the highest ideals and the noblest of dreams, but nothing works unless you do. It is not enough to *talk* about the successes you hope to achieve in the future. You have to put thoughts into action. Build structure into your day. It is in rituals and routines that we find momentum and motivation. Make selling a habit. Work daily at your success. Samuel Johnson said, "The chains of habit are generally too small to be felt until they are too strong to be broken."

Develop good work habits. Everyone needs some form of structure in his or her day. Stay focused and disciplined. Don't overindulge in idleness. Ask yourself this question: Is the time I spend watching television adding to my knowledge, my income, or my earning power — or is it adding only to my waistline? Use your time constructively and efficiently.

Spend an hour every day reading industry–related books. Keep abreast of changes in technology and in the general economy that impact your product. Stay current on technological and economic trends. Read sales guides to constantly improve your ability and skills. Your dedication to self–improvement will impact your sales results and will also enhance your professionalism.

Practice the Behaviour Modification Exercises at the end of each chapter. Do them repeatedly and look for improvements in the quality of your responses. Read the chapters frequently and practice using your body to enhance the level of your communication. Become fluent with your body language.

To be a leader in any profession takes dedication, time and countless hours of preparation. It is no different in sales. Your professionalism and success are within your control. That is why your accomplishments are so meaningful.

I will leave you with a quote from Edward A. Merten, "The usual outward characteristics of a successful salesperson are well known to all of us — neat appearance, good personality, fine speaking voice, *etc.* But it is the inner quality of 'drive' that is the most important but the least discernible. It is generally agreed that the priceless ingredient for success in selling is the desire to sell and the willingness to work hard at it."